What the World Eats

What the World Eats

Photographed by **Peter Menzel**   Written by **Faith D'Aluisio**

Tricycle Press
Berkeley

PUBLISHER'S NOTE:

All of the recipes in this book have been professionally tested. Due to the difficulty of acquiring certain ingredients in the United States, the following substitutions were made during testing: for the quandongs in Marge Brown's Quandong Pie (page 16), peaches; for the fresh pigskin in Dong Family's Pigskin Jelly (page 45), the skin only from skin-on pork belly pieces; for the mutton in Nadia Ahmed's Okra Tagin with Mutton (page 65), leg of lamb steaks; for the seal meat in Greenlandic Seal Stew (page 82), London broil; for the 10-pound live turkey in Susana's Turkey Soup (page 87), a 7$\frac{1}{2}$-pound dressed turkey; for the Anna d'Italie tomato paste, karite butter, smoked rice, and sumbala in Natomo Family Rice Dish (page 112), imported Italian concentrated tomato paste in a tube, canola oil, long-grain white rice with liquid smoke, and ground cumin, respectively; for the olive leaves in Alma Casales' Sopa de Jaiba (page 117), bay leaves; for the pimento berries and pig's knuckles in Hubert's Knuckle (page 135), whole allspice berries and pig's feet, respectively; and for the seasoned *comal* in Diana Fernandez's Quesadillas from Fresh Corn Tortillas (page 151), seasoned cast iron pot on the stove.

Photo on page 1: After going grocery shopping, Brian and Brianna Fernandez prepare to devour Texas-sized *pan dulces* in the back of the family minivan.

Photo on page 2: Steam rises in clouds from the huge woks of this noodle vendor in Kunming, in southwest China.

Photo on page 3: Diana Fernandez, her mother Alejandrina Cepeda, and Diana's kids Brian and Brianna prowl the local H-E-B supermarket in San Antonio, Texas.

Library of Congress Cataloging-in-Publication Data

Menzel, Peter, 1948-
What the world eats / photographed by Peter Menzel; written by Faith D'Aluisio.
p. cm.
Includes bibliographical references and index.
Summary: "A photographic collection exploring what the world eats featuring portraits of twenty-five families from twenty-one countries surrounded by a week's worth of food"—Provided by publisher.
ISBN-13: 978-1-58246-246-2
ISBN-10: 1-58246-246-1
1. Food—Pictorial works. 2. Diet—Pictorial works. 3. Food habits—Pictorial works. I. D'Aluisio, Faith, 1957- II. Title.
TX353.M438 2008
641.30022'2—dc22
2007041439

ISBN 978-1-58246-246-2

Printed in China

Cover and text design by Nancy Austin
Chart and graph design by Katy Brown

10 9 8 7 6 5 4

First Edition

Contents

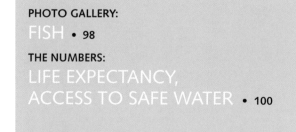

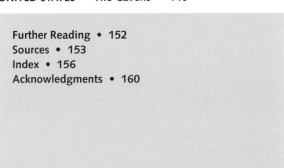

Glancing up at a visitor, Fourou—the twelve-year-old daughter of Soumana Natomo's second wife, Fatoumata—takes a momentary break from the family breakfast of thin rice porridge cooked with sour milk. Like most famlies in their village in Mali, the Natomos eat outdoors, sitting on low stools arond a communal pot in the courtyard of their house.

World on a Plate

Imagine for a moment that it is early Saturday morning in the United States. You have just awakened and it's time for breakfast. If yours is like the majority of American families, your meal might consist of one or more of the following: boxed, sweetened cereal with milk; bacon and eggs; pancakes; breakfast bars; and toaster pastries. Your food probably has been purchased by your parents in a nearby supermarket. You might have an idea of the basic ingredients of the food you're going to eat, but probably not. You move from your bed to the breakfast table and eat until you're full.

If, instead, you wake up in a village in the east African country of Chad, like Amna Mustapha, twelve (page 38), there are no boxes of ready-to-eat cereal, no cartons of milk, and no pastries from a supermarket bakery (in fact, there is no supermarket). You and your parents grow and raise the family's food. Your meal is always the same—puddinglike porridge called *aiysh* and a thin okra soup with maybe a bit of dried goat meat for added flavor. But before you can eat it, the sorghum or millet grain for the porridge must be pounded by hand or machine milled, the water for it pulled from a distant hand-dug well, the vegetables picked fresh or gathered from the drying shed, and the wood or dried cattle dung collected to fuel the cooking fire. Children do almost all of this work for the family, although the mother usually does the cooking. Everyone gathers around to dip pieces of *aiysh* into the soup and eat them with their hands. Then the children leave for the day to water and tend the animals.

If . . . you wake up in a village in the east African country of Chad, like Amna Moustapha . . . your meal is always the same— puddinglike porridge called "aiysh" and a thin okra soup with maybe a bit of dried goat meat for added flavor.

Amna's family is just one that we profiled, in twenty-one different countries, to explore humankind's oldest social activity: eating. How would one week's worth of food in Chad or India stack up against one week's worth in Greenland, Mexico, the United States, Egypt, or France? We decided to find out. At the end of each visit, we created a portrait of each family surrounded by a week's worth of groceries.

The global marketplace has changed the way people eat. In the suburbs of Paris, French teenagers stop at McDonald's for a quick bite and their parents shop at modern supermarkets. France's own brands of giant supermarkets, like the American Wal-Mart, are sprouting up across the planet. In urban China, such megamarkets are replacing the bustling farmers' markets and home gardens that for hundreds of years have provided the essentials of the Chinese diet. Traditional food and centuries-old eating habits are being replaced by "modern" energy-dense foods (like those modern breakfast foods you're eating this Saturday morning). As societies modernize and become wealthier, people become less physically active and actually need less food. Instead, people are eating more—and getting fat.

Even without reading the mountains of research that bear this out, the effects are easy to spot. Just look around. Many affluent countries are overfed. And, unfortunately, it seems that in developing countries, even before people attain a level of prosperity that helps ensure their adequate nutrition, they are eating in ways almost guaranteed to make them less healthy. Alma Casales, thirty-four (page 114), a young mother living in Mexico, is surprised to learn that the six gallons of Coca-Cola she, her husband, and her young children are drinking in the course of one week at all their meals and throughout the day is basically sugar water. In fewer than twenty years Mexico's population has moved from a rate of less than 10 percent overweight to over 65 percent.

As charitable organizations continue their campaigns against world hunger, others have started campaigns against world obesity. In the year 2000, the World Watch Institute reported that for the first time in human history there were just as many overfed people on the planet as underfed.

So back to Amna's breakfast in Africa, and yours in America. There is a mind-boggling number of variables to consider, but you may be surprised to learn that the breakfast in Africa could well be the more nutritious of the two. It is simply cooked and has no added fats, sugars, chemicals, or artificial ingredients. Also, the vegetables and grain didn't travel hundreds of miles to the breakfast table—only a few dozen steps.

Do some detective work to figure out the differences between your meal and Amna's. Read the labels and ingredient lists of the

The countries and regions profiled
in this book appear in red.

For this Sunday brunch outside Hamburg, Germany, Jörg Melander rode his bicycle through late-November snow to get rolls and pastries from a bakery near home. His wife Susanne has just finished an all-night nursing shift and is making the effort to enjoy the family meal, instead of going right to bed. But the bread, cheese, and jam washed down with tea, coffee, and hot chocolate are worth it.

In the Golden Horn area of Istanbul, Turkey, the Çinar family gathers on the floor of their small living room to share their morning meal: feta cheese, olives, leftover chicken, bread, rose jam, and sweet, strong tea.

As she arranges her clothes in the chilly desert dawn, D'jimia Ishakh Souleymane, a Sudanese widow at a refugee camp in neighboring Chad, watches the pot of water she is heating to make *aiysh* (porridge). Anticipating the new moon at the end of the month of Ramadan, when Muslims fast, she is preparing a celebratory meal for her five children.

foods you're planning to eat. There are some things you won't be able to discover—such as how far the bacon had to travel to get to your plate, or where the grain in your cereal was grown. Fresh fruit is easier to detect. In the modern supermarket, stickers on the fruit sometimes tell you that an apple is from New Zealand, seven thousand miles away. If you want bananas, you can get them any time of year, shipped from countries around the globe. Most of those bananas were picked long before they got ripe. Americans haven't had to worry about whether a certain food is in season for a long time because of the elaborate transportation system developed to supply supermarkets. In Amna's country, they get to eat fruit only when it ripens locally—juicy red watermelons available once a year.

* * * *

Why did we choose some countries and not others? Sometimes we covered a country because we were already there working on a different project; for others it was because we wanted to see something new. We covered some countries just to develop a good cross section of the world. Neither of us had been to Greenland, and we really wanted to see glaciers before they all disappear into the rising sea. It had been nearly twenty years since we worked in Ecuador, so we included this South American country to see how much it had changed. We wanted a third country in Africa, and to observe refugee life, so we traveled to Chad. And we wanted to see how Poland had survived its years of communism. We included three families in the United States to invite comparison. How do you think they compare to one another? Look at each of these families and compare your own family's weekly grocery list to theirs. Keep in mind, though, as you look at these photographs, that none of these families is meant to be a statistical representation of the country in which they live. They represent themselves, and even then as only a snapshot in time. I wrote the stories of all these families after extensive interviews and observation in each of the countries we visited plus additional questions afterward.

There are signs of change everywhere. Food has become a complicated business as companies compete in the global marketplace and fight for your food dollar. You have here a tool to help you understand a little more about the world around you. Bon appétit.

Australia THE BROWNS OF RIVERVIEW

The Brown family of Riverview, Australia, with a week's worth of food: Doug Brown, 54, and his wife Marge, 52, with their daughter Vanessa, 32, and her children, Rhy, 12, Nakayla, 15, John, 13, and Sinead, 5. The length of the Browns' grocery list changes depending on whether Vanessa and her children are living with them at the moment. Cooking methods: electric stove, microwave, and BBQ. Food preservation: refrigerator-freezer. Favorite foods—Doug: "Anything anyone else cooks." Marge: yogurt. Sinead: Mackas (McDonald's).

ONE WEEK'S FOOD IN JANUARY: 481.14 AUSTRALIAN DOLLARS/$376.45 USD

Grains and Other Starchy Foods: $28.79
Coliban variety potatoes, 8.8 lb
Home Brand (store brand) white bread, sliced, 4 loaves
Home Brand whole wheat bread, sliced, 2 loaves
Weet-Bix breakfast cereal, 2.7 lb
White Wings self-raising flour, 2.7 lb
basmati rice, 2.2 lb
Kellogg's Sultana Bran cereal, 1.9 lb
Nanda spaghetti, 1.1 lb
Nanda spirals, 1.1 lb
white pocket bread (pita), 13 oz
Kellogg's corn flakes, 10.9 oz

Dairy: $24.55
Sunshine whole milk, 2.4 gal
Home Brand vanilla ice cream, 1.1 gal
Home Brand thickened cream, 1.3 qt
margarine, 2.2 lb
Yoplait yogurt, nonfat, 1.5 lb
Yoplait Gogurt (drinkable yogurt), 1.2 lb
Kraft Cheese Singles, 1.1 lb

Meat, Fish, and Eggs: $117.99
Woolworths smoked ham, 11 lb
silverside (corned beef), 9.9 lb
minced meat, 6.6 lb
pork chops, 6.6 lb
sausages, 6.6 lb
steakettes, 6.6 lb
chicken, 4.4 lb
rissoles, 4.4 lb
Home Brand eggs, 24
Home Brand beef patties, frozen, 2.2 lb
Home Brand fish fingers, frozen, 2.2 lb

Fruits, Vegetables, and Nuts: $30.54
yellow bananas, 2.7 lb
white nectarines, 2.4 lb
Jarrahdale variety pumpkin, 2.4 lb
carrots, 2.2 lb
yellow onions, 2.2 lb
tomatoes, 2.1 lb
avocados, 3
cucumbers, 1.4 lb
Master Foods tomato sauce, 16.9 fl oz
zucchini, organic, 1.1 lb
mixed vegetables, frozen, 1.1 lb
red bell peppers, 11.2 oz

celery, 8.8 oz
green bell peppers, 8 oz
shallots, 6.4 oz

Condiments: $35.44
Cornwell's vinegar, 1.6 qt
Bundaberg white sugar, 2.2 lb
Holbrook's Worcestershire sauce, 25.4 fl oz
Kraft cheese spread, 1.1 lb
Cornwell's Lancashire relish, 1.1 lb
Master Foods BBQ sauce, 16.9 fl oz
IXL plum conserve (jam), 10.6 oz
Kraft Chilli and Lime Dressing, 10.2 fl oz
Kraft mayonnaise, 6.7 oz
Kraft smooth peanut butter, 6.6 oz
baking powder, 4.4 oz, used in johnnycakes
Mitani chicken salt, 3.5 oz
Keen's curry powder, 2.1 oz
mustard, 1.6 oz
Splenda (artificial sweetener), 1 oz
salt, 2.2 oz

Snacks and Desserts: $4.59
Smiths chips, variety pack, 14.1 oz
rich tea biscuits (traditional English cookies), 7.1 oz

Prepared Food: $4.28
Maggi instant beef noodles, 1.1 lb
Gravox gravy, 4.2 oz

Fast Food: $28.28
McDonald's: 6 Happy Meals, 3 Mc Oz (burgers),
    Coca-Cola, 6 small, 1 large

Beverages: $37.92
Frantelle spring water, 7.9 gal
diet *Coca-Cola,* 1.6 gal
Mildura fruit drink, 1.1 gal
Just Juice orange drink, 2.5 qt
diet *Sprite,* 2.1 qt
Golden Circle apple juice, 2.1 qt
Golden Circle lime cordial, 2.1 qt
Golden Circle orange and mango crush, 2.1 qt
Kirks club lemon soda squash, 1.3 qt
Kirks creaming soda, 1.3 qt
Kirks lemonade, 1.3 qt
Kirks pasito (passionfruit-flavored drink), 1.3 qt
Solo lemonade, 1.3 qt
Sunkist orange drink, 1.3 qt

Coca-Cola, 20.3 fl oz
Tetley tea, 175 teabags (this number is *not* a typo!)
Bushell's coffee, 1.8 oz

Miscellaneous: $64.07
Longbeach cigarettes, 10 packs
Winfield tobacco, 1.8 oz
Lion cigarette papers, 4 packs

FACTS ABOUT AUSTRALIA

Population of Riverview: 4,332

Land that is desert: 44%

Ratio of sheep to people: 5 to 1

Indigenous (native) population: 2.5%

Indigenous population in 1777: 100%

Greater life expectancy of nonindigenous versus indigenous population: 20%

Total annual health care expenditure per person in US$: $3,123

Kangaroos killed under commercial harvest for meat and skins (2003): 3,909,550

The vast Australian outback stretches for hundreds of miles.

Brisbane is a tropical city that has heavy thunderstorms almost every afternoon in the summer.

Five-year-old Sinead was terrified the first time she saw her mother slaughter a sheep. "She said to me, 'Mommy, I don't love you anymore,'" says Vanessa Stanton, "and I told her, 'Well Sinead, we're not going to eat anymore if I don't.'"

Although Australia had no sheep until the late eighteenth century, when European settlers began to import and raise them in large numbers, many of the country's original inhabitants came to embrace the shepherd's life. Sheep slaughtering is a common chore for people living in the outback—Australia's vast, desolate interior—and Vanessa Stanton learned it from her parents. Her mother, Marge Brown, says living in the outback is "as much a part of me as breathing."

Marge, a nurse who worked in a rural clinic, married Doug Brown, whose job was to shave the wool off sheep. The Browns raised their children, and many foster chil-

John remembers a time when the family was still living on the sheep ranch and he was sent to catch a porcupine for dinner. "A porcupine is a lot of work," says Doug. "Dig after it, run after it, clean it, hang it, cook it for hours. And just when you're ready to eat it, your friends show up, all wanting a leg each."

dren, on a sheep ranch with no running water or electricity. "We cooked on an open fire and washed our clothes in a forty-four-gallon drum," says Marge.

Today, the Browns live in Riverview, a small town on the outskirts of the coastal city of Brisbane, Queensland. Since Marge suffered a series of strokes, the grocery shopping, household chores, and cooking have been Doug's jobs. After a lifetime spent in the solitary outback (also called "the bush"), Doug too says he has trouble living in the modern world. "My ears start ringing when too many people get to talking around me," he says. Their daughter Vanessa, a frequent visitor and sometime houseguest since her mother's illnesses, is more skilled at living in both worlds. She and her children meld into and out of the household seamlessly, as many of the children have lived with their grandparents off and on since they were young.

Morning meals center around Doug's fresh fruit salad, but it's not a particularly healthy one. "I dice it up and then add cream and sugar," says Doug. "A *lot* of cream and sugar," adds Vanessa. All three of the adults have diabetes, though only Marge has to take medication to control it, and all are overweight. The Browns see being overweight as a common issue for many Australians: "Everyone here is looking for a quick way to lose weight," says Vanessa. "Queensland is the fat state. Southern Australians are slimmer. It's hotter up here—everyone runs for the air conditioner, and they lay there in front of the TV." "With Mackas, Sizzlers, and KFC," adds Doug. ("Mackas" is what Australians call McDonald's.) Doug tries to limit the fast-food trips to only once or twice a month, especially when the grandchildren are home, but Sinead is able to charm him into going more often.

PHOTOGRAPHER'S FIELD NOTE

The last time I was in Australia, I spent a week in the outback, camping with three grandmotherly aboriginal artists who showed me how to dig up and eat "witchetty" grubs (larvae of the cossid moth) and honey ants. We also ate a two-foot-long goanna lizard that one of them had killed with a spade, and a kangaroo tail they bought at a Quickstop. I learned a lot and admired the women for their ability to walk into the barren red desert and forage meal after meal.

Fast food wasn't always the family treat. John remembers a time when the family was still living on the sheep ranch and he was sent to catch a porcupine for dinner. "A porcupine is a lot of work," says Doug. "Dig after it, run after it, clean it, hang it, cook it for hours. And just when you're ready to eat it, your friends show up, all wanting a leg each." Everyone nods in agreement. "Once you have a porcupine in the house," adds Vanessa, "that's a big treat and you've got two or three families showing up for the johnny-cakes [wheat-flour campfire bread] and porcupine."

In the bush, porcupine, kangaroo, and lamb were standard food, but they play a smaller role in the family diet in suburban Brisbane. Disability payments from the government go directly into the adults' bank accounts every two weeks, and this money covers rent, meals, and expenses. "We've got to buy a certain amount of food, and it has

Every two weeks a new check appears and the family goes to the supermarket.

Breakfast during the children's summer vacation is low-key and unstructured. Everyone eats when the mood strikes them.

to last two weeks," says Marge. "In the bush, if we ran out of meat, it was easy to go over to the paddock and get a 'roo. Here, if you're out of money, you're out of meat."

Vanessa does feel that her children have missed out on some of the most basic experiences she remembers from her own childhood. "I had some loose tea and the kids couldn't believe it when I put the tea leaves in the water. They said, 'Where's the bags?' I asked them, 'Haven't you been educated in anything?'" Indeed they have: they are well aware of every branded soft drink, snack, and fast food. And they want them.

On the way back from Mackas (Aussie slang for McDonald's), 15-year-old Nakayla Samuals (in 50 Cent T-shirt) rips open the *Spy Kids* 3-D comic book that the restaurant awards to purchasers of Happy Meals. Like her half-sister Sinead Smith (drinking) and her friend Amelia Wilson, Nakayla is from an Aboriginal family whose roots lie in the arid outback. But the girls have little interest in outback cuisine; at least for now, Mackas is their culinary mecca.

Marge Brown's Quandong Pie

1 pound quandongs (bright-red wild Australian peaches),
    peeled, pitted, and chopped
1 cup sugar
1 tablespoon lemon juice
1 cup self-raising flour
3 cups all-purpose flour
6 ounces butter
$1/2$ teaspoon salt
1 cup milk

To make the filling, put the quandongs, sugar, and lemon juice into a saucepan and add water to cover. Cook at a low boil for 30 minutes. The water will turn red. Remove from the heat and drain in a colander, catching the liquid in a separate bowl. Put the liquid in the refrigerator to cool.

Preheat the oven to 350°F.

To make the pastry, work the flours, butter, and salt together in a bowl with your fingers (or use a metal dough blender). Add the milk and form into a ball. Roll out the pastry into two rounds big enough to cover a deep 8-inch pie dish. Fit one pastry round into the pie dish so that it just overlaps the edge.

Fill the prepared pie dish with the quandong mixture, adding 3 to 4 tablespoons of the reserved quandong liquid to moisten. Place the second pastry round over the filling and pinch the edges together. With a knife, cut small vent holes in the top. Decorate with leftover pastry bits (optional).

Put the pie in the preheated oven. Immediately lower the temperature to 300°F and cook for 30 to 60 minutes, until juices begin to bubble up. If the edges cook too quickly, cover with foil. Remove from the oven and let the pie rest for 10 minutes, then serve hot with custard, cream, or ice cream topped with some of the remaining quandong liquid.

John holds his sister Sinead as they graze in the nearly-empty refrigerator. But the next day, it's full—every two weeks a new check appears and the family goes to the supermarket.

In Shingkhey, a remote hillside village of a dozen homes, Nalim and Namgay's family assembles in the prayer room of their three-story earthen house with one week's worth of food for their extended family of thirteen. Cooking method: clay stove fueled by wood fire. Food preservation: natural drying. Family members (left to right, standing): Sangay Kandu, 39, husband of Sangay; Sangay, 35, holding Tandin Wangchuk, 7 months; Sangay Zam, 12, daughter of Sangay Kandu and Sangay; Chato Namgay, 14, monk, son of Sangay Kandu and Sangay; *(continued)*

ONE WEEK'S FOOD IN FEBRUARY: 224.93 NGULTRUM/$5.03 USD

Grains and Other Starchy Foods: $0.25**
red rice,* 66.2 lb • This also feeds the many guests who
    drop by at mealtimes.
flour,* 3.1 lb
red potatoes,* 2.2 lb
barley,‡ 2 lb, for toasting

Dairy:**
milk,* 2.8 gal, from family cows • Butter is churned from
    a portion of this milk; the by-product, whey, is also
    used. About 1.8 lb of cheese is produced from the milk
    as well.

Meat, Fish, and Eggs: $0.08**
eggs,*‡ 11
fish, dried, 4.4 oz • The family eats fish or meat—normal-
    ly in dried form—once or twice a month. Dried beef is
    eaten more often than fish. The fish in the photograph
    represents about three months' worth of either fish or
    meat. The dollar amount represents what the portion
    they eat in one week costs.

Fruits, Vegetables, and Nuts: $1.46**
mandarin oranges, 3.5 lb
yellow bananas, 1.4 lb
radishes, 6.6 lb
spinach,* 5 large bunches
mustard greens,* 4 large bunches
eggplant,* 2.2 lb
red onions, 2.2 lb
tomatoes, 1.1 lb
carrots,‡* 1.1 lb
green chile peppers, fresh, 4.4 oz, amount in photo repre-
    sents about three months' worth
red chile peppers, dried, 4.4 oz • Amount in photo
    represents about four months' worth. Normally all veg-
    etables are homegrown or borrowed from a neighbor.
    Vegetables and fruits are purchased infrequently.

Condiments: $1.27**
mustard oil,* 2.1 qt
salt, 3.3 lb, for cooking and feeding to cows for increased
    milk production
ginger, 1.1 lb
bicarbonate of soda (baking soda), 1 small pack, used to
    neutralize acid in tea
chile powder, 1 handful

Beverages: $0.76
tea rounds, 2 cakes, for butter tea
Red Label tea, 0.7 oz, for guests only • Water comes in
    through a plastic hose from a spring above the house
    and is used for cooking and boiled for drinking.

Miscellaneous: $1.21
betel nuts, 80
leaves for betel nuts, 2 bundles
lime paste, 1 pack

*Homegrown
‡Not in photo
**Market value of homegrown foods, if purchased
    locally: $29.06

Chato Geltshin, 12, son of Sangay Kandu and Sangay; (left to right, seated): Zekom, 9, daughter of Nalim and Namgay; Bangam, also called Kinley, 21, daughter of Nalim and Namgay; Drup Chu, 56, brother of Nalim; Choeden, 16, daughter of Sangay Kandu and Sangay; Nalim, 53, family matriarch and wife of Namgay; Namgay, 57, family patriarch and husband of Nalim; Geltshin 9, son of Sangay Kandu and Sangay.

PHOTOGRAPHER'S FIELD NOTE

Friends, neighbors, relatives, wandering photographers—visitors are always welcome at the earth-walled house of Namgay and Nalim. Anyone who shows up at the door is offered toasted rice and tea with milk or butter tea. Most visitors seem to wander in at mealtime and stay for the huge pot of steaming red rice prepared by Nalim and her daughter Sangay. On top of the rice, guests ladle chilies, cheese, vegetables (tomatoes, turnips, onions), and sometimes pieces of dried beef or fish. Sitting cross-legged in front of the hearth, everyone chats and shares stories, tossing and spitting inedible pieces of meat or bone onto the floor, which is patrolled by cats and chickens.

Namgay (left, by fire) and his wife Nalim (right, by fire) eat a lunch of red rice and a small cup of cooked vegetables with their family and friends in the kitchen area of their earth-walled house.

On this early winter morning in the Himalayan village of Shingkhey, a pot full of red rice simmers atop the low earthen stove in Nalim's kitchen. Nalim's grown-up daughter Sangay, a pleasant-faced woman with a ready smile, pushes another stick of wood into the fire hole to regulate the heat under the rice. Sangay's baby, Tandin Wangchuk, watches from his perch on her back as she mixes up whole chilies, cheese, onion, chile powder, and salt and grinds it into a curry paste to eat with the rice. Sangay's five other children and her two younger sisters are still asleep on the floor of the next room.

Meanwhile, Nalim has churned the morning milk into butter and is now preparing butter tea, which is butter, with a few tea leaves, in hot milky water. Her husband, Namgay, limps over to the kitchen fire and sits by the glassless window of their house, where he slurps his tea deeply and looks out over their small sleeping village. The quiet will end abruptly when the children awaken.

Nalim, who like most people in Bhutan has no family name, is a farmer who, with help from her family, grows most of the family's food here in the central part of the small kingdom of Bhutan, just northeast of India. Her husband Namgay is the village seer, or mystic; he spends his days reading holy Buddhist texts for the sick, the unlucky, and the hopeful. He also mills grain for other villagers, using a small fuel-powered machine that he got through a government loan program. Because he is disabled, Namgay can't do the heavy labor that most men in farming families do. That work is left to Nalim's son-in-law, Sangay Kandu, and Nalim's brother, Drup Chu, who do the plowing with a pair of stubborn bulls and a wooden plowshare. When they need extra help, others in the village pitch in—and Sangay Kandu returns the favor when asked: cooperation is often the key to survival in poor places.

Sangay and Nalim take turns tackling the inevitable tasks of parenthood and farming. One feeds breakfast to their family of thirteen, gets the kids ready for school, slops the pigs, and sends the cows off to graze, while the other heads to the fields for the day's work—sowing, hoeing, and harvest.

Like many Himalayan villages, Shingkhey has narrow, terraced fields, with trails between them that lead to earth-walled houses. Villagers work together to build the houses. Moist earth is shoveled into forms by men and boys and then pounded and compressed by women and girls. An overhanging roof on all four sides protects a house from bad weather. The houses are all three stories tall and

Above the municipal market, a shopkeeper's TV satellite dish doubles as a dehydration rack for red chili peppers.

have hand-carved windows—some with glass, most without—and an elaborately decorated prayer room. Painted by monks in traditional decorations and containing an ornate carved altar, the prayer room is used during the yearly *puja* (ritual family blessing) and for daily Buddhist offerings. Families live on the second story of the house; they store dried meat, grain, and straw in the large top-story loft, and their animals are corralled on the ground floor. For years, the government has been trying to stop families from keeping animals so close to their living quarters, because it encourages the spread of insects and disease, but it's still a common practice.

After the children get up, they fold up their bedding without being asked, and Zekom, the youngest daughter of Nalim and Namgay, distributes bowls in a circle on the wood floor. The wood has developed a handsome, waxy, hand-rubbed sheen after decades of being cleaned after meals of red rice, chilies, and cheese. Everyone accepts a bit of curry in a bowl, then rolls the rice into little balls and dips them into the curry. The conversation is brisk until the last scrap of food is eaten.

Young market vendors tend their family's cabbage, tomatoes, and onions in the Sunday market in Wangdi Phodrang, a two-hour walk from Shingkhey village.

In addition to rice, Nalim's family grows wheat, barley, and mustard. Farming the scattered, steeply pitched plots is hard work. Next to the house they raise tomatoes, carrots, spinach, chilies, green onions, beans, squash, and turnips. When they're not in school, the younger children are responsible for keeping animals out of the vegetable garden.

On the ledge of their house (left), Sangay, holding Tandin Wangchuk, watches government workers complete the electrical connections from a new small hydroelectric dam in a neighboring valley. The next day (below), during a celebration of the electrification, visiting officials join Namgay (at the head of the table) at a buffet of red rice, potatoes, tomatoes, cucumbers, beef, chicken, and a spicy cheese and chili pepper soup. The villagers have been stockpiling food for the event.

Almost all the family's meals consist of cheese, vegetables, and red rice. As Buddhists, they don't kill animals for food, but if a cow dies by accident, then they'll eat it. "When we have meat, we'll eat it until it's gone. It's morning, afternoon, and evening, meat," says Nalim, laughing. Otherwise, they have meat only during the *puja*, when a group of visiting monks cleanses the house of evil spirits. Every house in a village has a *puja* once a year and shares the meat of a pig, which has been killed by a special butcher. In Nalim's village of twelve houses, that's a taste of pig twelve times a year.

Sangay's daughter Choeden, sixteen, is the only child in the family who doesn't go to school. The chief animal-tender and field assistant, she is being groomed to take over the household and the farming. Originally this role was to be filled by Nalim's middle daughter, Bangam, but the girls decided the matter themselves: Choeden didn't want to go to school and Bangam did, so they switched. Nalim expects Bangam to use her education to get a job and help support the family. "There are so many people to feed, but so few people to do the work," says Nalim. "I hope that this will change as they get older."

Change comes slowly to the village, but it does come. Yesterday, Sangay went to the ledge outside their house and watched government

workers raise the last power pole to bring electricity to the area. In the evening before their dinner of red rice, chilies, and spinach curry, lit only by the kitchen fire, the family stood in the smoky room as a bare, dangling light bulb—the first in their home—came to life in the middle of the ceiling. The grins on their faces, bathed in this new, day-prolonging, artificial light, were wondrous.

The day after the electrifying celebration in the village, life returns to normal (above). Singing as they walk, Bangam (third from right) joins other village girls in collective women's work: cleaning out the manure from the animal stalls under the houses and spreading it on the fallow fields before the men plow. All wear the traditional *kira* worn by all Bhutanese women—a rather complicated woven wool wrap dress. Mean wear a robelike wrap called a *gho*.

Preparing to host visitors (left), Sangay pours a pot of tea into a thermos. Her half-sister Bangam holds the sieve. Meanwhile, Namgay, the family patriarch, waits patiently for a cup.

Bosnia and Herzegovina THE DUDOS OF SARAJEVO

The Dudo family in the kitchen-dining room of their home in Sarajevo, Bosnia and Herzegovina, with one week's worth of food. Standing between Ensada Dudo, 32, and Rasim Dudo, 36, are their children (left to right): Ibrahim, 8, Emina, 3, and Amila, 6. Cooking methods: electric stove, coal/wood stove. Food preservation: refrigerator-freezer.

ONE WEEK'S FOOD IN JANUARY: 334.82 KONVERTIBILNA MARKA/$167.43 USD

Grains and Other Starchy Foods: $17.40
bread, 15.5 lb
flour, 4.4 lb
potatoes, 4.4 lb
white rice, 2.2 lb
jufka (thin pastry sheets), 1.1 lb
Fiamma Vesuviana penne, 1.1 lb
Fiamma Vesuviana riso (pasta), 1.1 lb
pastry sheets, 1.1 lb
Embi corn flakes, 13.2 oz

Dairy: $17.77
milk, 1.9 gal
yogurt, drinkable, 1.1 gal
cream, 1.6 qt, used on bread or with eggs
Zvijezda ghee (butter clarified by boiling and converted
    into an oil), 2.2 lb
gouda cheese, 1.3 lb
travnicki cheese (white Bosnian cheese), 1.3 lb
butter, 1.1 lb
Iparlat lemon yogurt, 14.1 oz
Paschal pineapple yogurt, 14.1 oz

Meat, Fish, and Eggs: $54.22
ground beef, 4.4 lb
eggs, 30
hot dogs, 4 lb
chicken, baked, 2.2 lb
beef sausage, 2.2 lb
mutton, 2.2 lb
steak, 2.2 lb
veal, 2.2 lb
Argeta chicken pâté, canned, 1.1 lb
hard sausage, 1.1 lb
Sarajevo keep-long sausage, dried, 1.1 lb
sardines, canned, 8.8 oz

Fruits, Vegetables, and Nuts: $28.18
tangerines, 8.8 lb
apples, 6.6 lb
oranges, 6.6 lb
yellow bananas, 3.3 lb
lemons, 1.1 lb
figs, dried, 7 oz
cabbage, 2 heads
carrots, 2.2 lb
garlic, 2.2 lb
kidney beans, 2.2 lb
leeks, 2.2 lb
lentils, 2.2 lb
yellow onions, 2.2 lb
spinach, 2.2 lb
tomatoes, 2.2 lb
mushrooms, 1.1 lb
pickles, 1.1 lb
red chile peppers,‡ 1.1 lb
peanuts, 2.2 lb

Condiments: $8.75
sugar, 4.4 lb
sunflower oil, 1.1 qt
fruit compote,‡ 1.1 lb
cream, 8.5 fl oz, for coffee
Hellmann's mayonnaise, 8.3 oz
peach marmalade, 7.8 oz
mustard, 7.1 oz
sea salt, 7.1 oz
white sugar cubes, 3.5 oz
salt, 1.1 oz

Snacks and Desserts: $21.74
raisins, 4.4 lb
hard candy, 2.2 lb
Dominos milk chocolate candy, 1 lb
Tops orange and chocolate cookies, 1 lb
Nussenia nut cream (chocolate spread like *Nutella*), 14.1 oz
Mars candy bars, 5.9 oz
Gold Flips corn puffs, 4.2 oz

Prepared Food: $2.47
chicken soup mix, 5.5 oz
chicken bouillon, 4.7 oz

Homemade Food:
cake, whole, made with ingredients listed above

Beverages: $16.90
Fanta orange soda, 2 2.1-qt bottles
Coca-Cola, 2.1 qt
Dijamant mineral water, 2.1 qt
Frutti blueberry juice concentrate, 2.1 qt
Power of Nature blueberry and grape juice, concentrate,
    2 1.1-qt cartons
Sunset orange juice, 2.1 qt
Mljeveni coffee beans, 1.1 lb
cocoa, 8.8 oz
Dona pineapple juice concentrate, 8.5 fl oz
orange juice drinks, powdered, 5.3 oz
Nescafé instant coffee, 3.5 oz
tea, 3.5 oz

‡Not in photo

nsada Dudo sets tiny coffee cups on a tray as her husband Rasim gives a final brisk turn to the crank on his small brass coffee grinder. They are preparing strong, sugary, Turkish-style coffee for guests on this snowy Saturday afternoon in Sarajevo. She serves the coffee with two Turkish treats: *Rahat lokum,* nutty jellied chews (Turkish delight), and *halva,* a confection traditionally made from honey and ground sesame seeds. The Turkish influence is no surprise as Turkish forebears ruled much of southeastern Europe for centuries. The goodies attract Emina, three, and Amila, six, until they discover they aren't chocolate. The girls return to the window to watch their brother Ibrahim, eight, sledding with friends on new-fallen snow. "They love desserts," says Ensada, "so I bake on the weekends."

Despite their love of the long Sarajevan coffee break, neither Ensada nor Rasim has much leisure time. Ensada works long hours for a Muslim humanitarian organization, and Rasim is a private taxi driver in a city with too many taxi drivers trolling about for fares. The two return home at lunchtime for what is typically the main meal of the day. Despite Ensada's busy schedule, she does not rely on prepared foods or takeout for the lunchtime meal. She makes stewed chicken or *bosanski lonac*—a meat and vegetable stew usually made with mutton. The Dudos are Muslim and therefore eat no pork. Their evening meal is light and might include leftovers along with *ajvar,* a preserved eggplant and red pepper spread, on slices of crusty bread.

Although Ensada and Rasim buy most of their nonperishables at a bright new supermarket, they still prefer to buy eggs, seasonal

FACTS ABOUT BOSNIA AND HERZEGOVINA

Population of Sarajevo: 380,000 (est.)

Undernourished population: 9%

Total annual health care expenditure per person in US$: $198

Consumption of sugar and sweeteners per person per year: 73 pounds

Unemployment rate (2002): 45.5%

Ensada graciously welcomes visitors with Turkish sweets and cups of Turkish-style coffee on a handcrafted tray—metalwork is a Sarajevan specialty.

fruits, and vegetables at the outdoor Green Market Ciglane. Its surrounding area is a daily reminder of Bosnia's violent civil war of the early 1990s—the site of the 1984 Winter Olympics, with its great athletic feats, has become, in part, a graveyard full of the war dead.

Throughout the civil war, Ensada and Rasim Dudo struggled to feed their family. Women, children, and the elderly braved snipers' bullets to stand in line for water rations and to find food, while able-bodied men went to the front lines to fight. Public utilities and services were nonexistent. The task of survival completely took over daily life.

Today the Dudo family still lives in the same house Rasim's father built before the war. They say

Signs of the four-year siege of Sarajevo (former Serb gun emplacements overlooking the city; above) are still obvious today. Although food stalls have returned to the Ciglane market (left), parts of the Olympic park behind it have become a burial ground for siege victims.

the war-torn city is being rebuilt physically, but for many of the older people, who remember what life was like before the war, the emotional scars are slower to heal. Still, when their visiting grandmother watches Ibrahim and his friends happily sledding down the snow-covered hill outside their house, it helps her look to the future with more happiness than she might have otherwise.

KITCHENS

Chemically altering plant and animal tissue by exposing it to heat is one of the oldest practices in human culture, and certainly one of the practices that most distinguishes humans from our fellow creatures. Although the kitchens in these images are wildly different in location and appearance, all of them form the center of a home, if only temporarily. The kitchen is both a family gathering point and the place where a culture is at its most evident—whether a quick stir-fry between trains over a makeshift stove between railroad tracks or the baking of a chicken in a brand-new housing complex in Dubai.

Kouakourou, Mali

Breidjing Refugee Camp, Chad

Dubai, United Arab Emirates

Montreuil, France

Manila, Philippines

Bargteheide, Germany

Tingo, Ecuador

Copenhagen, Denmark

Although the kitchens in these images are wildly different in location and appearance, all of them form the center of a home, if only temporarily.

TOTAL POPULATION, URBAN POPULATION

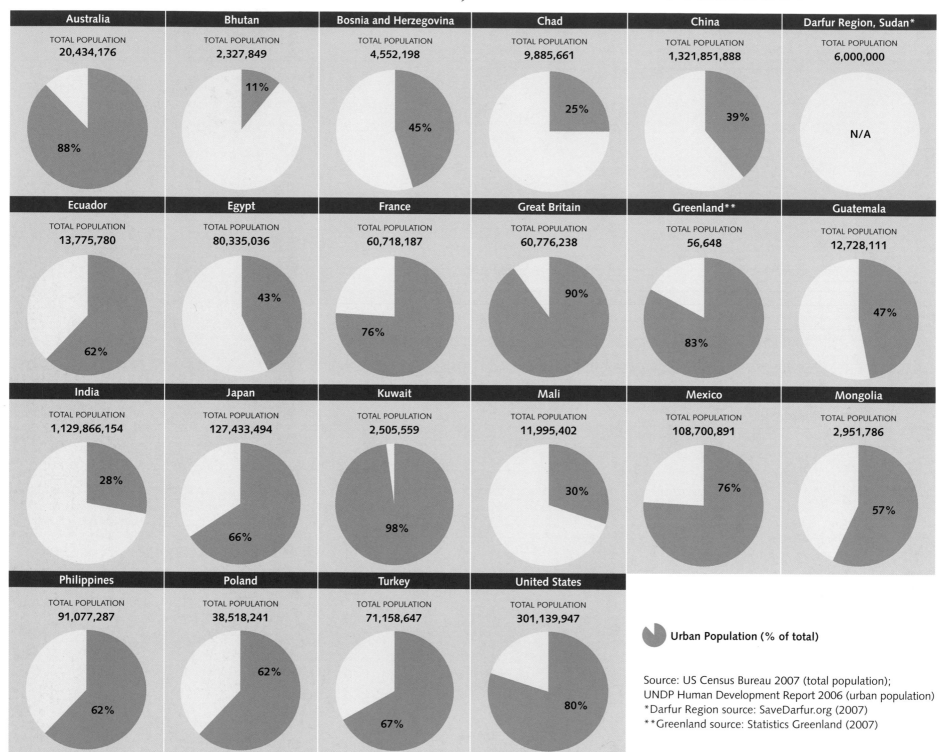

Australia	Bhutan	Bosnia and Herzegovina	Chad	China	Darfur Region, Sudan*
TOTAL POPULATION 20,434,176	TOTAL POPULATION 2,327,849	TOTAL POPULATION 4,552,198	TOTAL POPULATION 9,885,661	TOTAL POPULATION 1,321,851,888	TOTAL POPULATION 6,000,000
88%	11%	45%	25%	39%	N/A

Ecuador	Egypt	France	Great Britain	Greenland**	Guatemala
TOTAL POPULATION 13,775,780	TOTAL POPULATION 80,335,036	TOTAL POPULATION 60,718,187	TOTAL POPULATION 60,776,238	TOTAL POPULATION 56,648	TOTAL POPULATION 12,728,111
62%	43%	76%	90%	83%	47%

India	Japan	Kuwait	Mali	Mexico	Mongolia
TOTAL POPULATION 1,129,866,154	TOTAL POPULATION 127,433,494	TOTAL POPULATION 2,505,559	TOTAL POPULATION 11,995,402	TOTAL POPULATION 108,700,891	TOTAL POPULATION 2,951,786
28%	66%	98%	30%	76%	57%

Philippines	Poland	Turkey	United States
TOTAL POPULATION 91,077,287	TOTAL POPULATION 38,518,241	TOTAL POPULATION 71,158,647	TOTAL POPULATION 301,139,947
62%	62%	67%	80%

Urban Population (% of total)

Source: US Census Bureau 2007 (total population);
UNDP Human Development Report 2006 (urban population)
*Darfur Region source: SaveDarfur.org (2007)
**Greenland source: Statistics Greenland (2007)

AREA IN SQUARE MILES, POPULATION DENSITY

Australia
AREA IN SQUARE MILES
2,967,124
(slightly smaller than
the contiguous 48
U.S. states)

POPULATION DENSITY
7

Bhutan
AREA IN SQUARE MILES
18,142
(half the size of Indiana)

POPULATION DENSITY
128

Bosnia and Herzegovina
AREA IN SQUARE MILES
19,736
(slightly smaller than
West Virginia)

POPULATION DENSITY
230

Chad
AREA IN SQUARE MILES
495,624
(slightly more than
three times the size
of California)

POPULATION DENSITY
20

China
AREA IN SQUARE MILES
3,704,426
(slightly smaller than the
entire United States)

POPULATION DENSITY
357

Darfur Region, Sudan
AREA IN SQUARE MILES
170,000
(slightly larger
than California)

POPULATION DENSITY
35

Ecuador
AREA IN SQUARE MILES
109,454
(slightly smaller
than Nevada)

POPULATION DENSITY
126

United States
AREA IN SQUARE MILES
3,794,083

POPULATION DENSITY
79

Turkey
AREA IN SQUARE MILES
301,304
(slightly larger
than Texas)

POPULATION DENSITY
236

Poland
AREA IN SQUARE MILES
120,696
(slightly smaller than
New Mexico)

POPULATION DENSITY
319

Philippines
AREA IN SQUARE MILES
115,800
(slightly larger
than Arizona)

POPULATION DENSITY
786

Egypt
AREA IN SQUARE MILES
386,560
(slightly more than
three times the size
of New Mexico)

POPULATION DENSITY
208

France
AREA IN SQUARE MILES
211,154
(slightly less than twice
the size of Colorado)

POPULATION DENSITY
302

Great Britain
AREA IN SQUARE MILES
94,500
(slightly smaller
than Oregon)

POPULATION DENSITY
643

Greenland
AREA IN SQUARE MILES
836,109
(slightly more than three
times the size of Texas)

POPULATION DENSITY
0.1

Population Density = People Per Square Mile

Mongolia
AREA IN SQUARE MILES
603,749
(slightly smaller
than Alaska)

POPULATION DENSITY
5

Mexico
AREA IN SQUARE MILES
761,404
(slightly less than three
times the size of Texas)

POPULATION DENSITY
143

Mali
AREA IN SQUARE MILES
478,640
(slightly less than twice
the size of Texas)

POPULATION DENSITY
25

Kuwait
AREA IN SQUARE MILES
6,879
(slightly smaller
than New Jersey)

POPULATION DENSITY
364

Japan
AREA IN SQUARE MILES
145,844
(slightly smaller
than California)

POPULATION DENSITY
874

India
AREA IN SQUARE MILES
1,269,010
(slightly more than
one-third the size of
the United States)

POPULATION DENSITY
890

Guatemala
AREA IN SQUARE MILES
42,032
(slightly smaller
than Tennessee)

POPULATION DENSITY
301

Washington, Oregon, Montana, North Dakota, Minnesota, Idaho, Wyoming, South Dakota, Wisconsin, Michigan, Maine, Vermont, New Hampshire, New York, Massachusetts, Rhode Island, Connecticut, Nevada, Utah, Nebraska, Iowa, Pennsylvania, New Jersey, California, Colorado, Kansas, Illinois, Indiana, Ohio, Maryland, Delaware, Washington DC, West Virginia, Virginia, Missouri, Kentucky, North Carolina, Arizona, New Mexico, Oklahoma, Arkansas, Tennessee, South Carolina, Alabama, Georgia, Mississippi, Texas, Louisiana, Florida, Alaska, Hawaii

Source: CIA World Factbook (2007)

Chad THE ABOUBAKARS OF BREIDJING REFUGEE CAMP

The Aboubakar family of Darfur province, Sudan, in front of their tent in the Breidjing Refugee Camp, in eastern Chad, with a week's worth of food. D'jimia Ishakh Souleymane, 40, holds her daughter Hawa, 2; the other children are (left to right) Acha, 12, Mariam, 5, Youssouf, 8, and Abdel Kerim, 16. Cooking method: wood fire. Food preservation: natural drying. Favorite food—D'jimia: soup with fresh sheep meat.

ONE WEEK'S FOOD IN NOVEMBER: 685 CFA FRANCS (COMMUNAUTÉ FINANCIÉRE AFRICAINE)/$1.22 USD

Grains and Other Starchy Foods:**
sorghum ration, unmilled, 39.3 lb
corn-soy blend ration (CSB), 4.6 lb

Dairy:
not available to them

Meat, Fish, and Eggs: $0.58**
goat meat, dried and on bone, 9 oz
fish, dried, 7 oz
Note: Periodically, such as at the end of Ramadan, several
families collectively purchase a live animal to slaughter
and share. Some of its meat is eaten fresh in soup and
the rest is dried.

Fruits, Vegetables, and Nuts: $0.51**
limes, small, 5
pulses ration, 4.6 lb, the seeds of legumes such as peas,
beans, lentils, chickpeas, and fava beans
red onions, 1 lb
garlic, 8 oz
okra, dried, 5 oz
red chile peppers, dried, 5 oz
tomatoes, dried, 5 oz

Condiments: $0.13**
sunflower oil ration, 2.1 qt
white sugar ration, 1.4 lb
dried pepper, 12 oz
salt ration, 7.4 oz
ginger, 4 oz

Beverages:
water, 77.7 gal, provided by the international aid group
Oxfam, and includes water for all purposes; rations
organized by the United Nations with the World Food
Programme

**Market value of food rations, if purchased locally: $24.37

At the end of the month of Ramadan, the Muslim fasting
period, some of the families in D'jimia's block celebrated
the festival of Eid al-Fitr by banding together to buy a
goat, which they then slaughtered. While the meat simmered in a soup, many refugees went to services at an
improvised mosque.

Sunrise at the refugee camp. Another day of waiting begins.

D'jimia Ishakh Souleymane awakens before dawn on this hot November morning and steps carefully around her children sleeping on the tent floor. She pulls on a fold of bright purple fabric to cover her head and shoulders, in accordance with Muslim custom, and then opens the flap to ready her outdoor kitchen for the first meal of the day. Three rocks set in a triangle prop the family pot above a tiny wood fire. Tilting forward on a low, rickety stool, she scoops handfuls of milled sorghum from a small sack and stirs it into a pot of boiling water. When the mixture is a thick porridge, she dumps the cooked grain into an oiled bowl and swirls its surface flat. Next, she makes soup from a handful of dried tomatoes, some salt, and water. She turns the now-congealed cereal—called *aiysh*—onto a plate and takes the soup pot off the fire. Now, breakfast for six is ready outside her tent in the dusty, sprawling Breidjing Refugee Camp.

Across this camp and dozens of others in Chad and Sudan, tens of thousands of Sudanese refugee women just like D'jimia are stooped over their pots in front of their tents, cooking virtually the same food for breakfast, lunch, and dinner. All are living in the same situation—in a country not their own, and far from where they ever imagined they'd be. Civil war in Sudan, Africa's largest country, has been waged for over fifty years. Refugee camps like Breidjing have been set up to house civilians driven from their homes by the latest violent clashes. The camps in Chad are beset at every turn by harsh weather, lack of enough world aid, disease epidemics, sanitation problems, and water shortages.

Registered families get a tent, a blanket, a bucket, soap, and food from the aid organizations that run the camps. Per person, per day, the rations are 15 ounces of cereal, such as sorghum or millet; 1 tablespoon of sugar; 1 teaspoon of salt; and slightly less than ¼ cup each of pulses (such as lentils), CSB (a corn-soy blend, either sweet

Sitting near the food distribution center right after sunrise, a refugee woman patiently sifts through the sand to pluck out any bits of grain that might have dropped to the ground during the previous day's ration disbursement.

The arrival of an Oxfam water truck is an instant call for everyone in the camp to show up with a container. The trucks fill yellow waterbed-like bladders, which rest on low platforms. The water flows through buried pipes to water distribution centers.

or salty), and vegetable oil. The total equals about 2,100 calories, less than the recommended daily minimum for an active sixteen-year-old, but more than enough for a toddler still drinking breast milk. Rations are the same for each individual; decisions about who eats more or less are made within each family. But many refugees said, "We're still hungry every day." The hunger may be as much for home as it is for fresh vegetables, fruit, milk, and meat.

The food D'jimia prepares here is the same food she prepared at home, and she prepares it the same way—just in smaller amounts. Daughter Acha, a quiet, smiling twelve-year-old, knows how to cook this traditional fare. "She watched me and learned, as I learned to make it from my mother," says D'jimia. The girl's primary tasks, though, are to help with the younger children, gather firewood, and fetch water.

When evening comes, D'jimia cooks again. Her son Abdel Kerim carries his soup and *aiysh* to the tent of the assistant chief and eats

FAMILY RECIPE

D'jimia Ishakh Souleymane's Aiysh
(Congealed Porridge)

1/2 *coro* (approximately 1 pound) millet flour
1 *coro* (approximately 2 quarts) water
Vegetable oil (enough to coat aiysh)

Bring the millet to a mill to grind. After obtaining the ground millet flour, light the fire and bring the water to a boil in a pot. Add the millet flour in small amounts, until it begins to thicken and bubble. Stir constantly, pulling the mixture toward you in the pot until it holds together in a gelatinous mass.

Oil a bowl and press the mixture into it to make a round shape; flatten the top. Invert onto a serving plate or tray.

Squatting before the fire with her children, D'jimia Souleymane stirs a pot of *aiysh*, the thick porridge that this refugee family eats three times a day.

with him and his sons. A boy of sixteen is considered a man and therefore too old to eat with his mother and the other children. D'jimia watches the remaining four children dip pieces of *aiysh* into a thin okra soup and reminisces about home. "We were in perfect peace and had plenty of food," she says. "We had everything sufficient in our village—very different from here. We had animals, and we were farming. Every day we had fresh meat." She also had a cow for milk and ten big mango trees. D'jimia would sell her extra fruit and root vegetables at her village market and could afford to buy the children clothes, candies, and school supplies. Staying busy was part of the joy of living—now, living in a refugee camp as a guest, it is impossible.

Through all the turmoil and tumult, a bright spot for D'jimia is the camp school, run by the aid organizations. The children are in school here, just as they were in her village. "Education will help the children find work and be secure," she says, though she's not exactly sure how. A man has come around to her tent today to collect 200 CFA francs (36 cents, USD) per child for school supplies. Though it's all the money she has, she gives it to him—an investment in the future.

PHOTOGRAPHER'S FIELD NOTE

Housing and feeding thirty thousand people in a remote and forbiddingly harsh landscape hundreds of miles from the nearest paved road is no small matter. When we visited Chad in late 2004, the refugee crisis was full-blown. These refugees couldn't go home to Sudan, couldn't leave, and weren't supposed to stay. Nor could they farm, herd cattle, or build a permanent house. Every day was exactly the same. In their outdoor prisons, no one was malnourished, but no one was well fed, either.

Water is a constant preoccupation in the refugee camp. Every day, lines of women and children carry jugs and pots of drinking and cooking water from distribution points to their tents.

Chad THE MUSTAPHAS OF DAR ES SALAAM VILLAGE

The Mustapha family in their courtyard in Dar Es Salaam village, Chad, with a week's worth of food. Gathered around Mustapha Abdallah Ishakh, 46 (turban), and Khadidja Baradine, 42 (orange scarf), are Abdel Kerim, 14, Amna, 12 (standing), Nafissa, 6, and Halima, 18 months. Lying on a rug are (left to right) Fatna, 3, granddaughter Amna Ishakh (standing in for Abdallah, 9, who is herding), and Rawda, 5. Cooking method: wood fire. Food preservation: natural drying.

ONE WEEK'S FOOD IN NOVEMBER: 10,200 CFA FRANCS (COMMUNAUTÉ FINANCIÉRE AFRICAINE)/$18.33 USD

Grains and Other Starchy Foods: **
millet,* 4 coro (a *coro* is a Chadian unit of volume approximately equal to 2 qt)
millet flour,* 3 coro
sorghum,* 3 coro

Dairy: **
milk,* 7 coro, from family cows

Meat, Fish, and Eggs: $2.16 **
chickens,* 8.8 lb meat, after cleaning
goat meat, dried on the bone, 6.6 lb

Fruits, Vegetables, and Nuts: $7.19 **
watermelons, 22 lb
harar (squash), 17.6 lb
dates, 1 coro
okra,* dried, 1 coro
red onions,* 1 coro
garlic,* 0.5 coro
tomatoes,* dried and milled, 0.5 coro
red chile peppers,* dried and milled, 0.3 coro
peanuts,* 3 coro

Condiments: $8.54
peanut oil, 1.1 gal
sugar, 0.5 coro
salt, 0.5 coro

Beverages: $0.44
tea, 3.5 oz
water, for both drinking and cooking

*Homegrown
**Market value of homegrown foods, if purchased locally: $25.44

FACTS ABOUT CHAD

Population of Dar Es Salaam: 210 (estimate)

Population that is subsistence farmers and cattle herders: over 80%

Land planted in permanent crops: 0.02%

Population with access to safe water: 42%

Years of ethnic warfare endured since gaining independence from France in 1960: 35

Total annual health care expenditure per person in US$: $20

Physicians per 100,000 people: 4

Undernourished population: 33%

Households with access to electricity: 2%

McDonald's, Burger King, KFC, Pizza Hut restaurants: 0

As the sun rises, two men perform their morning prayers beneath a tree in the village of Dar Es Salaam in central Chad.

To water their animals, Amna Mustapha (left) and a cousin must first dip plastic containers into a six-foot well (behind Amna). They then pour the water into a low earthen-walled pool from which the animals drink.

When the children arrive at the *wadi*, the socializing doesn't stop but the nonsense does; the boys back off and the girls begin to repair the shallow earthen watering troughs. They must be rebuilt each day before the herds arrive. The sun beats down on their covered heads as they pull buckets of water from the narrow wells that have been dug into the *wadi*, then dump the water into the troughs for the small herds of cows and goats that will be brought here to drink. When the girls finish their work, they fill their jugs with the day's drinking and cooking water. Within minutes, Amna's brothers and cousins arrive with the family's herd. The girls then splash water onto their hot

Twelve-year-old Amna Mustapha and her cousin Fatna tie gourds and plastic jugs to the wooden saddles on their fathers' donkeys, then hoist themselves up for the morning ride across the plain of east central Chad to fetch the day's water. There are no arguments about whose turn it is to go—children here learn at a young age what's expected of them, and there's no room for argument if everyone wants to eat.

When Amna and Fatna join twenty or thirty other chattering children, mostly girls, for the twenty-minute ride to the *wadi*, a seasonal riverbed that's dry this time of year, they're on donkey-autopilot. Not even the boys on horse- and camelback, who gallop up, then stop in a cloud of dust to tease the girls, can deter their forward motion.

faces and head home with the cooking water; the cows and goats, left behind with their herders, begin the daily struggle to find something green to eat. Although there are some schools in the village and the main towns in Chad, the Mustapha children don't attend one. Education takes on greater importance once people see that education is going to mean money for the family. This is not even remotely the case for rural Chadian children like the Mustaphas, who need to help with the family's land and animals to survive.

Although surrounded by livestock, Amna's father, Mustapha Abdallah Ishakh, and his family eat red meat infrequently. When they do eat it, they rarely slaughter an animal from their herd because that would deplete their assets. Instead, they split the cost of an animal purchased from the local market with several families and butcher it for feasts like the celebration at the end of the Muslim holy month of Ramadan. When the family has meat, Mustapha's wife Khadidja dries some and later adds it to the soup that family members eat with their thrice-daily porridge called *aiysh*. Milk, too, is scarce; Mustapha's cows aren't big milk producers because there isn't much around for them to eat. Khadidja is able to extract only about enough for a cup of curds a day after the scrawny calves have suckled; she adds it to the soup, dividing the milk among nine people.

Wadis in this part of Chad are dry nine months of the year. During that time, villagers must dig down to the water, shoring up the wells with millet stalks to keep them from collapsing. It's hard work: the water rapidly evaporates, sinks into the sand, and is drunk by the animals, and the girls have to keep refilling the pools.

Khadidja Baradine begins her morning by scooping an ember from the previous night's fire onto a handful of straw to start a cooking fire.

Although there are some schools in the village and the main towns in Chad, the Mustapha children don't attend one. Education takes on greater importance once people see that education is going to mean money for the family. This is not even remotely the case for rural Chadian children like the Mustaphas, who need to help with the family's land and animals to survive.

China THE DONGS OF BEIJING

The Dong family in the living room of their one-bedroom apartment in Beijing, China, with a week's worth of food. Seated by the table are Dong Li, 39, and his mother, Zhang Liying, 58, who eats with them a few times a week. Behind them stand Li's wife, Guo Yongmei, 38, and their son, Dong Yan, 13. Cooking method: gas stove. Food preservation: refrigerator-freezer. Favorite food—Dong Yan: *yuxiang rousi*, fried shredded pork with sweet and sour sauce.

ONE WEEK'S FOOD IN JULY: 1,233.76 YUAN/$155.06 USD

Grains and Other Starchy Foods: $6.52
Xiaozhan rice (a type of rice grown in China), 11 lb
white bread, 2 loaves
French bread, 2 baguettes

Dairy: $26.29
Bright yogurt, plain, 2.1 qt
Bright milk, whole, 1.1 qt
Häagen-Dazs ice cream, assorted flavors, 11.4 oz
butter, unsalted, 7.1 oz
Häagen-Dazs vanilla ice cream, 5.5 oz
Häagen-Dazs vanilla almond ice cream, 3 oz

Meat, Fish, and Eggs: $26.97
flatfish, 3 lb
beef flank, 2.4 lb
pigs feet, 1.8 lb
beef shank, 1.3 lb
chicken wings, 1.3 lb
eggs, 9
beef, marinated in soy sauce, 1 lb
salmon, fresh, 9.8 oz
pig's elbows, 8.6 oz
sausage links, 7 oz
sirloin steak, 5.3 oz

Fruits, Vegetables, and Nuts: $16.45
cantaloupe, 6 lb
oranges, 4.2 lb
firedrake fruit (sweet-flavored cactus fruit), 2.3 lb
lemons, 1.5 lb
plums, 1.1 lb
tomatoes, 2.4 lb
cucumbers, 2.3 lb
cauliflower, 1 head
celery, 1.4 lb
carrots, 1 lb
taro, 13.8 oz
cherry tomatoes, 13.4 oz
long beans, 10.6 oz
white onions, 10.6 oz
shiitake mushrooms, dried, 8.8 oz
shiitake mushrooms, fresh, 5.6 oz
black fungus (agaric), 3.5 oz

Condiments: $17.26
Luhua peanut oil, 1.1 qt
Hojiblanca olive oil, 16.9 fl oz
soy bean juice, 16.9 fl oz
orange jam, 12 oz
hot pepper sauce, 9.7 oz
salad dressing, 7.1 oz
white sugar, 7.1 oz
Maxwell House coffee creamer, 6.7 oz
sesame oil, 6.8 fl oz
BB sweet hot sauce, 5.6 oz
citron day lily, 5.3 oz, dried flower bud used for flavoring
honey, 5.3 oz
vinegar, 5.3 fl oz, eaten with boiled dumplings
pepper paste, 3.5 oz
sour cowpeas (black-eyed peas), preserved, 3.5 oz
seafood sauce, 3.4 fl oz
Knorr chicken-flavored MSG (monosodium glutamate,
    a flavor enhancer), 1.8 oz
MSG, 1.8 oz
salt, 1.8 oz
curry powder, 0.4 oz

Snacks and Desserts: $17.70
snack chips, 7 bags
Ferrero Rocher chocolates, 14.1 oz
Xylitol gum, 1 bottle
Dove chocolate, 8.5 oz
Xylitol blueberry gum, 3 packs
Xylitol gum, 3 packs

Prepared Food: $6.12
sushi rolls, packaged, 1.1 lb
eel strips, baked, 8.2 oz
Knorr chicken bouillon, 0.7 oz

Fast Food: $9.17
KFC: 2 chicken hamburgers, 2 chicken burritos
4 *Coca-Cola*, medium
2 packages French fries

Beverages: $27.95
grapefruit juice, 2.1 gal
Asahi beer, 6 12-fl-oz cans
Bright orange juice, 2.1 qt
Tongyi orange juice drink, 2.1 qt
Coca-Cola, 3 12-fl-oz cans
Great Wall dry red wine, 25.4 fl oz
diet *Coca-Cola*, 12 fl oz
Jinliufu rice wine, 8.5 fl oz
Nescafe instant coffee, 3.5 oz
tap water, boiled for drinking and cooking

Miscellaneous: $0.63
Zhongnanhai cigarettes, 1 pack

More than a hundred KFC outlets operate in Beijing alone.

Chinese street food stands sell an extraordinary variety of treats. Under the salesman's outstretched hand is a rack of skewered scorpions.

Dong Li and his wife, Guo Yongmei, are part of the new breed of Beijinger, moving into China's developing middle class. Rather than live a life dictated by centuries of culture and tradition, Chinese like the Dongs want to mold their own lives. Although the central Communist government still keeps an eye on the people, its grip on their daily lives has loosened.

Dong Li, who works for the Beijing municipal government, and Guo Yongmei, who is a bookkeeper, live in Beijing's Chaoyang District. Their only child, Dong Yan, thirteen, is a quiet, studious boy. As an only child—China has long enforced a one-child-per-family policy—he gets the undivided attention of his parents and grandparents. Dong Li's mother, who retired ten years ago from an electronics factory, has cared for her only grandson since he was a baby. When she stops by for a visit, we ask her what she thinks about her son's modern apartment. "It's not really to my taste," she says. "There is nothing here that is familiar." But she smiles as she says this.

Like most urban Chinese, the Dongs enjoy a combination of traditional Chinese food, Western fast food, and international cuisine. They don't shop much at the smaller markets anymore, instead choosing chain hypermarkets that stock the international brands that are now flowing into the country. A foreign visitor will notice immediately that the multinational hypermarkets have tailored their stores to Chinese tastes. The seafood counter turns out to be an aquarium-like fish and seafood emporium much like those found in the outdoor markets in many Chinese cities. There are swimming fish, shellfish, slithery eels, fish on ice, cases of live crabs, and frozen fish pieces. Guo Yongmei and Dong Li make their choices together. "Thirty years ago," says Dong Li, there was very little food. "Now there is a lot, and it tastes better." He and Guo Yongmei eat at restaurants once a week or so, but even then they mostly go to Chinese

FACTS ABOUT CHINA

Population of Metro Beijing: 15,380,000

Total annual health care expenditure per person in US$: $70

Population, age 20 and older, with diabetes: 2.4%

Consumption of sugar and sweeteners per person per year: 15 pounds

Number of KFC restaurants in 2007: 1,800

Population living on less than $2 a day: 47%

Number of days of curing after which a "thousand-year-old egg" is most delectable: 100

restaurants. Dong Yan is more apt to want Western fast food. "There is a McDonald's near my school," he says. "I go with my friends." He eats there a couple of times a week—more often if he can. His favorite fast food, though, is KFC. Does he eat different foods than his parents do? "I like more sweet foods that my parents don't really like." "He's growing up differently than I did," says his father. And it's clear from his voice that Dong Li's happy about it. He's hoping that his son grows up to be a linguist, so that he can travel and study in different countries. But at thirteen, Dong Yan is not inclined to commit to his future.

Dong Family's Pigskin Jelly

1 pound fresh pigskin, hair scraped off
1 scallion, cut into 6 or 7 pieces
1-ounce piece ginger, peeled, cut into 3 or 4 pieces
4 cloves garlic, whole
$1/2$ ounce Sichuan peppercorns (Asian prickly ash), whole
1 whole star anise, broken into 4 or 5 pieces
2 teaspoons Chinese cooking wine
Salt
Soy sauce
1 teaspoon vinegar

Put the pigskin into a pot with water to cover and bring to a boil for a short time to soften. Remove the pigskin and cut into 1- to 2-inch strips to facilitate handling.

Combine the pigskin, scallion, ginger, 2 cloves of the garlic, the peppercorns, star anise, and wine. Add water to cover and bring to a medium boil.

When the water boils, add salt and soy sauce to taste. Continue to boil until the pigskin is extremely tender.

Remove all the condiments and spices with chopsticks, but leave the pigskin in the liquid. Remove from the heat; when cool, store in the refrigerator.

To serve, crush the remaining 2 cloves of garlic. Take the cooled pigskin strips from the liquid and cut them into bite-size pieces. Mix with the crushed garlic, the vinegar, and salt and soy sauce to taste.

In many restaurants and markets in China, much of the seafood is sold live (below) as a guarantee of freshness. In other ways, the supermarket hews closely to Western models, right down to the workers offering samples (above).

China THE CUIS OF WEITAIWU VILLAGE

The Cui family of Weitaiwu village, Beijing Province, in their living room with a week's worth of food. Seated (left to right): Cui Lianyou, 59; his wife, Wu Xianglian, 61; their son, Cui Haiwang, 33, and his wife, Li Jinxian, 31; Haiwang's grandmother, Cui Wu, 79; and Haiwang and Jinxian's son, Cui Yuqi, 6. Cooking methods: gas burner, coal stove. Food preservation: refrigerator-freezer. Favorite foods—Cui Yuqi: fish, Li Jinxian: vegetables, Wu Xianglian: "anything," Cui Wu: "everything."

ONE WEEK'S FOOD IN JULY: 455.25 YUAN/$57.27 USD

Grains and Other Starchy Foods: $3.98**
wheat flour, 23.2 lb
white rice, 6.6 lb
cornmeal, 2.2 lb
millet, 2.2 lb
potatoes,* 2.2 lb

Dairy: $1.26
milk, whole, 2.1 qt.

Meat, Fish, and Eggs: $23.27
lamb, 11 lb
eggs, 44
pork, 6.7 lb
chicken, 4.4 lb

Fruits, Vegetables, and Nuts: $11.84**
watermelons, 18.3 lb
muskmelons (cantaloupe), 12 lb
white peaches, 6.6 lb
black grapes, 3.3 lb
green apples, 3.3 lb
plums, 3.3 lb
pears, 1.1 lb
cucumbers,* 15.5 lb
green beans, 5.5 lb
eggplant, 4.4 lb
tofu, 4.4 lb
cabbage, 2 heads
cauliflower, 1 head
chives,* 3.3 lb
tomatoes, 3.3 lb
zucchini,* 3.3 lb
celery, 2.2 lb
garlic, 2.2 lb
green bell peppers, 2.2 lb
corn,* 5 ears
Weiwei soymilk powder, 1.2 lb
carrots, 1.1 lb
black fungus (agaric), 8.8 oz
green onions,* 8.8 oz

Condiments: $5.57
peanut oil, 2.8 lb
soy sauce, 21 fl oz
sesame oil, 11.8 fl oz
ginger, 1.1 lb
Longfei vinegar, 1.1 lb
salt, 1.1 lb
white sugar, 8.8 oz
cilantro (Chinese parsley), 1 bunch
white pepper, 1.8 oz
yeast, 1.4 oz
five-spice powder, 0.4 oz
MSG, 0.4 oz
Sichuan peppercorns (Asian prickly ash), 0.4 oz
star anise, 0.2 oz

Prepared Food: $0.09
chicken bouillon, 1.8 oz

Beverages: $6.73
Yanjing beer, 12 21.3-fl-oz bottles
Coca-Cola, 2.1 qt
Sprite, 2.1 qt
rice wine, 1.1 lb
jasmine tea, 5.3 oz
water for drinking and cooking, pumped from the
   family well

Miscellaneous: $4.53
Hongmei cigarettes, 10 packs

*Homegrown
**Total value of homegrown foods, if purchased locally:
   $1.96

FACTS ABOUT RURAL CHINA

Rural population (people/households):
   800 million/245 million

Population of Weitaiwu village: 450 (estimate)

Laborers in China engaged in agricultural
   work: 50%

Population with access to safe water in rural/
   urban areas: 67/93%

Population with access to safe sanitation in
   rural/urban areas: 28/69%

Ratio of percentage of rural to urban population
   that is overweight: 1 to 2.3

Ratio of rural to urban electricity use per person:
   1 to 2.1

Ratio of rural to urban household consumption:
   1 to 3.5

Average per-person income, rural/urban
   (in US$): $444/2,321

Number of refrigerators per 100 families, rural/
   urban: 12/80

Rural residential energy consumption that
   comes from noncommercial sources like
   straw, paper, dung: 57%

Ratio of Internet users in rural/urban areas:
   1 to 3.3

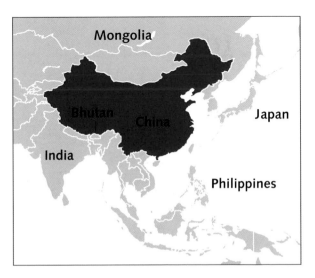

Li Jinxian always likes to buy fruit from the same vendor, a woman whom she has gotten to know.

On the half-mile walk from home to his cornfield, Cui Lianyou greets neighbors who are working, lounging, eating, and visiting along the single concrete road in Weitaiwu, a rural village sixty miles east of Beijing. Food has traditionally played such a central role in Chinese life that it is often invoked even in day-to-day greetings. "*Chi fan le ma?* (Have you eaten?)" one farmer might say to another when they meet. "*Chi bao le* (I'm full)," his friend replies.

Cui Lianyou turns down a small path, past the new chemical fertilizer plant, and hops onto one of the narrow, raised ridges of earth that separate the villagers' fields from one another. After a short distance, he steps into his own densely planted cornfield—the stalks tall now, with plump yellow ears that will soon be ready for picking. Grandfather Cui also grows barley, wheat, soybeans, and peanuts, depending on the season. Land assignments—made at the local government level—are temporary. Most recently the six members of the Cui family were awarded half a *mu* each, for a total of three *mu* (slightly more than half an acre)—much less than the amount they used to have.

Grandfather Cui's wife, Wu Xianglian, and their daughter-in-law Li Jinxian grow tomatoes, cabbage, squash, and cucumbers in their courtyard kitchen garden, and grapes on a trellis, but despite the family's plots of land, they manage to grow only about 10 percent of what they need all year. The rest of their food is purchased with money earned by Li Jinxian's husband, Cui Haiwang, who is a printing press repairman working out of Beijing. He would prefer to stay with his family in the village, but there are no jobs at which he can earn enough to support them. He comes home on the weekends. Li Jinxian sometimes works at a nearby factory that makes clothing for Japan and the United States. She is paid 20 yuan ($2.50 USD) for a ten-hour workday and dislikes the job. The family considers itself poor in comparison with the rest of their village, but they still have some of the amenities that disposable income brings—a TV, a stereo system, a phone—and their family compound has been refurbished within the last two years.

Like most of the Chinese population, the Cuis let nothing go to waste. Cornhusks are fed to their three sheep. They also eat a portion of the corn crop. The trio was purchased as lambs and when full grown will be sold to the local butcher to provide the family with extra income.

Does Grandfather Cui have a favorite food? "Pork," he says. Then, "No, pork and lamb. And beef." Finally, he summarizes: "Meat! I like meat!" His wife laughs at him as she passes by on her way to another of her many household tasks—"There's nothing we won't eat," she retorts, and Grandfather Cui agrees. He recalls the Cultural Revolution, a period in Chinese history in the 1960s and 1970s, when the country devolved into social, political, and economic chaos, causing great food shortages. "Back [...then], we ate anything we could find. We dug up everything, even wild grass. And if food fell on the ground, it didn't matter—just pick it up, brush it off, and eat it. We didn't waste *anything*!"

The desire of typical rural Chinese to eat only traditional foods

Loaded down with groceries for the family portrait, Li Jinxian and Cui Haiwang are met by Grandfather Cui with his *salun che* (three-wheeled cart) at the entrance to the narrow lane leading to their home. The Cui family—indeed, most rural Chinese—would never buy this quantity of food at one time, but would buy smaller quantities every day.

is changing with Cui Yuqi's generation. "For his birthday, we buy him foods he wants [but] we don't eat, like butter and cake," says Grandfather Cui, who has never eaten anything but food prepared in the Chinese manner by his mother and his wife. No one in the family has ever tasted cheese. Cui Yuqi likes packaged snacks and candy, and although he has never had Western fast food, he's looking forward to trying some. His mother says that she too would try it, but says so apprehensively. His grandparents say they wouldn't eat it even if it were affordable.

Though her husband works out of Beijing, the rest of the family has visited the massive city only once—it's geographically close, but too expensive. The big city overwhelmed the older folks, but "Cui Yuqi was fascinated," says his mother. She's sure that he, at least, will go there again.

Breakfast at the Cuis' (above) includes fresh eggs from the family hens and hot *mian tiao* (noodles) with a little cooked spinach and MSG (monosodium glutamate, a flavor enhancer). The round chopping block is made from a thick slice of tree trunk. In the courtyard that morning (right), Li Jinxian husks corn from their cornfield under the watchful eye of Great-grandmother Cui Wu. The family will eat some of the corn and trade the rest; the husks go to the sheep. Two hours later, lunch is ready (left). Six-year-old Cui Yuqi reaches for a piece of smoked chicken in the family's kitchen house. Other foods on the table include (clockwise from bottom) cauliflower and beef; pig's feet; dried tofu curd and cucumber; cucumber and beef; steamed egg-white custard; stir-fried green peppers and beef. The tomatoes in the center were picked from their kitchen garden that morning.

FAST FOOD

Has any human invention ever been both as loved and as hated as fast food? Feelings run deep about the huge U.S. fast-food chains, especially McDonald's and KFC. Internationally recognized as symbols of Americanization, globalization, and overflowing schedules, they are also symbols of convenience, reliability, and (usually) cleanliness. Food activists from Paris to Pretoria like to denounce fast food, but the pressures that give rise to it won't go away with a manifesto. Perhaps a backlash movement will arise, prompting equally convenient yet healthier alternatives.

Beijing, China

Warsaw, Poland

Manila, Philippines

Tokyo, Japan

San Antonio, Texas, USA

Beijing, China

Raleigh, North Carolina, USA

Moscow, Russia

Shanghai, China

NUMBER OF MCDONALD'S RESTAURANTS

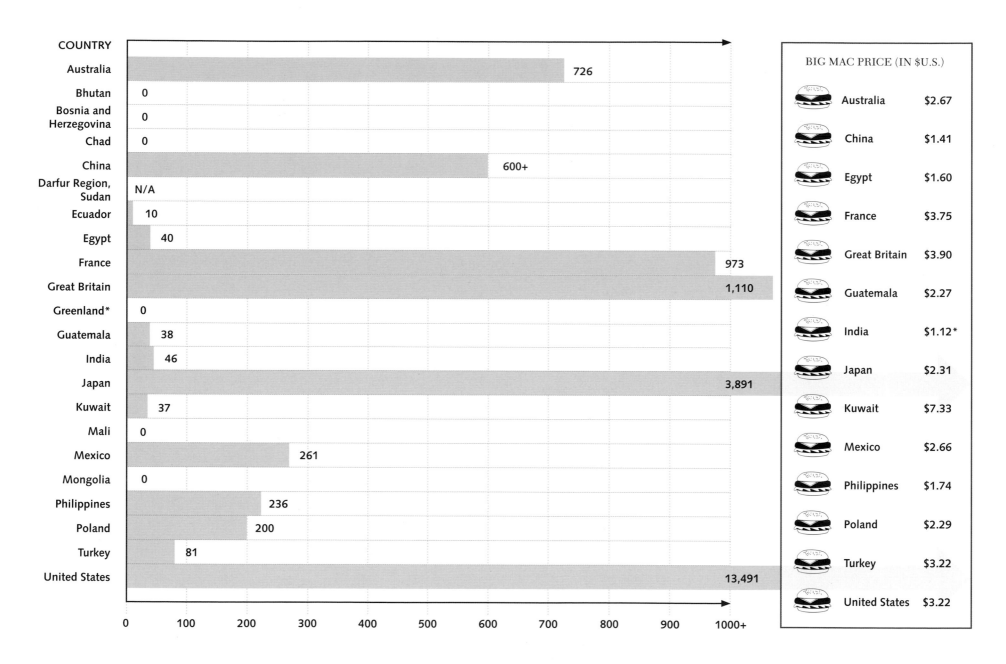

COUNTRY	Number of Restaurants
Australia	726
Bhutan	0
Bosnia and Herzegovina	0
Chad	0
China	600+
Darfur Region, Sudan	N/A
Ecuador	10
Egypt	40
France	973
Great Britain	1,110
Greenland*	0
Guatemala	38
India	46
Japan	3,891
Kuwait	37
Mali	0
Mexico	261
Mongolia	0
Philippines	236
Poland	200
Turkey	81
United States	13,491

BIG MAC PRICE (IN $U.S.)	
Australia	$2.67
China	$1.41
Egypt	$1.60
France	$3.75
Great Britain	$3.90
Guatemala	$2.27
India	$1.12*
Japan	$2.31
Kuwait	$7.33
Mexico	$2.66
Philippines	$1.74
Poland	$2.29
Turkey	$3.22
United States	$3.22

Source: *The Economist* Big Mac Index (2007) and www.McDonalds.com

N/A = Information not available

*Chicken Maharaja Mac; no beef in India's Big Mac

OVERWEIGHT POPULATION, OBESE POPULATION

COUNTRY	Overweight (% of total population)		Obese (% of total population)	
	male	female	male	female
Australia	74	64	24	25
Bhutan	35	44	6	14.5
Bosnia and Herzegovina	57	51	14	22
Chad	12	19.5	0.3	1.7
China	34	24.5	1.6	1.8
Darfur Region, Sudan	N/A	N/A	N/A	N/A
Ecuador	42	52.5	7	17
Egypt	65	75	22	24.5
France	47	35	8	6.8
Great Britain	67	63	22	24.5
Greenland*	35	33	16	22
Guatemala	58	66	16	30
India	17	15.5	1.2	1.4
Japan	27	18	1.8	1.5
Kuwait	70	80	30	52.5
Mali	15	34	0.5	6
Mexico	68	67.5	24	34.5
Mongolia	52.5	69	8.5	29.5
Philippines	21	29	1.5	4
Poland	52.5	45	13	18
Turkey	48	67	10.5	32
United States	75	73	37	42

Source: World Health Organization Global InfoBase Source Metadata (estimate for 2005)
N/A = Information not available
*Greenland source: Correspondence with Chief Medical Officer (2003)

UNITED STATES

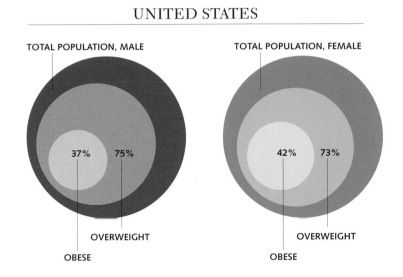

CHAD

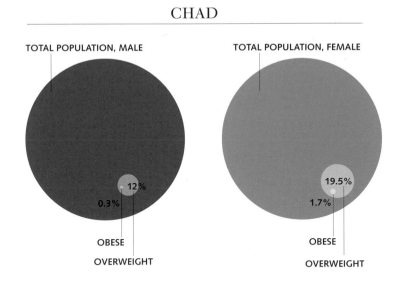

Ecuador THE AYMES OF TINGO

The Ayme family in their kitchen house in Tingo, Ecuador, a village in the central Andes, with one week's worth of food. Ermelinda Ayme Sichigalo, 37, and Orlando Ayme, 35, sit flanked by their children (left to right): Livia, 15; Natalie, 8; Moises, 11; Alvarito, 4; Jessica, 10; Orlando *hijo* (Junior, held by Ermelinda), 9 months; and Mauricio, 30 months; Not in photograph: Lucia, 5, who lives with her grandparents to help them out. Cooking method: wood fire. Food preservation: natural drying.

ONE WEEK'S FOOD IN SEPTEMBER: $31.55 USD (ECUADOR ADOPTED THE U.S. DOLLAR AS ITS OFFICIAL CURRENCY IN 2000)

Grains and Other Starchy Foods: $17.40**
white potatoes, 100 lb
white rice, broken, 50 lb, cheaper than whole rice
ground wheat,* 15 lb
corn flour, 10 lb
white flour, fine, 10 lb
green pea flour, 8 lb
white flour, coarse, 6 lb
Note: The Aymes normally grow their own potatoes and
    corn but have none to harvest at this time of year.
    They have eaten the last of their homegrown barley.

Dairy:**
milk, 1.8 gal, from family cows • Only part of the week's
    supply is shown in the photograph.

Meat, Fish, and Eggs: none.

Fruits, Vegetables, and Nuts: $11.25
plantains, 13.4 lb
yellow bananas, 6.2 lb, purchased overripe as they are
    cheaper that way
oranges, 3.6 lb
lemons, 2.5 lb
Andean blackberries, 1 lb
lentils, 10 lb
carrots, 3.6 lb
red onions, 3 lb
leeks, 2 lb
lettuce, 1 head

Condiments: $2.90
brown sugar, 11 lb, purchased as a cake, used for sweeten-
    ing coffee and eaten as candy
salt, 1.5 lb
vegetable oil, 16.9 fl oz
cilantro, 1 bunch

Beverages:**
stinging nettle, 1 small bunch, gathered wild for tea
corn silk, 1 handful, boiled in water for both tea and
    medicine
water from a nearby spring, carried by hand, for drinking
    and cooking

*Homegrown
**Market value of homegrown foods, if purchased: $3.20

Wearing a traditional Andean felt hat, Ermelinda spends part of her morning in the windowless cooking hut, cleaning barley in the light from the doorway. After she blows away the dust and chaff, the grain is ready to be ground for breakfast porridge.

It's no surprise that Ermelinda Ayme Sichigalo would rather leave her children at home in Tingo, their small village in the central Andean highlands, than bring them down the mountain to the weekly market in the much bigger town of Simiatug. Her youngest children, especially, want everything they see, and she has little money for extras. With eight children to raise—including the baby riding in a sling on her back—plus doing field work, tending a flock of sheep, cooking, doing the laundry and the marketing, as well as practicing midwifery and medicinal healing, Ermelinda doesn't have much time to indulge the children. Even without little children tagging along, the Aymes' food forays aren't easy. There are no shops or markets in Tingo—only neighbors and family to borrow from and share with. The hike down the steep mountain from Tingo to Simiatug is three miles long; then there's the walk back.

The Ayme family's fields are eleven thousand feet up in the mountains, far removed from Ecuador's rich tropical lowlands. "Our land is dry, and the wind is harsh," says Orlando, "so it's not that good for planting. The land farther down is much more fertile, but it's too expensive." Despite the difficult climate, they manage to live through most of the year on what they grow in their fields: potatoes, *oca* (a root vegetable), corn, wheat, broad beans, and onions. The only animal protein they eat is guinea pig and chicken, and that only a few times a year. They have a milk cow that produces about one quart a day.

Food security comes in the form of their other enterprise—their flock of fifty sheep, which the Aymes own jointly with their extended family. They raise the animals not for food, but to sell in the market—to tide them over during the dry season, when there's little or nothing to harvest. This week they're selling two sheep at the Simiatug market to buy food.

The valley town of Simiatug, accessible only by means of a long, winding dirt road and hillside trails, is the sole food-shopping destination for everyone within a thirty-mile radius. The descending figures in bright-red ponchos that dot the mountains signal the arrival of market-bound Ecuadorians, the Aymes included. The animal market is a social gathering spot—mostly for the men, who catch up on the week's events while hoping to sell their animals. Orlando accepts $35 for his sheep—not as much as he wanted, but enough to go shopping.

Making the long return trip from the weekly market in the valley, Orlando Ayme leads his father-in-law's horse.

In Simiatug, a man ties a 100-lb. bag of potatoes onto his wife's back.

Ermelinda buys food at the cooperative market.

The Aymes always buy their most important staple foods first, and then they keep spending until the money is gone. Fresh fruits and vegetables, last on the shopping list, are purchased only if there's extra money. They buy carrots, leeks, onions, and some fruit today, because they sold the sheep. Then the money is gone, so the shopping is over. Orlando lashes as much food as he can onto the horse he borrowed from his father-in-law, and they carry the rest up the mountain themselves.

By the time they get home, the wind is howling outside and it's almost dark. Ten-year-old Jessica, who has been out on her own with the sheep all day, has corralled them for the night in their makeshift pen and left the dog there to scare off wild animals. In the kitchen house (the family has two small adobe huts, one for the kitchen, the other for sleeping), Ermelinda kindles the embers to bring the fire to life.

Ermelinda adjusts the wood so that the embers remain at a constant temperature for cooking—much like a modern stove, except without the knobs. There's no ventilation in the cooking house, so the ceiling beams and walls are black with soot. The room is warm but smoky. There are no appliances, no clocks, no furniture, no running water, and no modern kitchen utensils.

No one has to be called for dinner. Even the eldest daughter, Livia, who has been doing schoolwork in the family's sleeping house, has appeared. Everyone sits on the dirt floor or on little benches and eats their fill of the starchy soup they have most nights.

PHOTOGRAPHER'S FIELD NOTE

On five previous trips to Andean countries in South America, I had failed to partake of the biggest delicacy the Andes has to offer: *cuy* (guinea pig). I had seen the creatures in the kitchens of rural highland dwellings, where they have the run of the house and yard. On this trip I went to a storefront restaurant called Salon Los Cuyes II (loosely translated, "Guinea Pig Hall II"). The guinea pigs were the biggest I'd ever seen—the size of small dogs. Cooked whole on the rotisserie, they were like big dachshunds with fat rat heads, complete with protruding incisors and crispy rodentlike ears. The light-pink *cuy* meat, served with a traditional potato, onion, and peanut-sauce stew, was delicious. It tasted like a cross between suckling pig and rabbit and was just as rich; three of us shared half a *cuy* and still couldn't finish it.

Cultivating potatoes on a windy afternoon, Ermelinda wraps her baby in two shawls tied in different directions. When she and Orlando arrived at the field, a ten-minute walk from their home, they said a quick prayer to Pacha Mamma (Mother Earth) before working the land. Occasionally, Ermelinda has to adjust the baby's position, but generally she has no problem carrying her tiny passenger.

A three-hour drive over dirt roads from the Aymes' house in Tingo, Zumbagua has a vegetable market big enough to attract a few tourists.

Egypt THE AHMEDS OF CAIRO

The Ahmeds' extended family in the Cairo apartment of Mamdouh Ahmed, 35 (glasses), and Nadia Mohamed Ahmed, 36 (brown headscarf), with a week's worth of food. With them are their children, Donya, 14 (far left, holding baby Nancy, 8 months); Karim, 9 (behind bananas); Nadia's father (turban); Nadia's nephew Islaam, 8 (football shirt); Nadia's brother Rabie, 34 (gray-blue shirt); his wife, Abadeer, 25; and their children, Hussein, 4; and Israa, 18 months (held by family friend).

ONE WEEK'S FOOD IN MAY: 387.85 EGYPTIAN POUNDS/$68.53 USD

Grains and Other Starchy Foods: $2.73
potatoes, 8.8 lb
white rice, 6.6 lb
basbousa powder (semolina flour and ground nut mix),
    2.2 lb, used to make a dense, Egyptian cake saturated
    with syrup
macaroni, 2.2 lb
pita bread, 2.2 lb
gullash (paper-thin dough), 1.1 lb

Dairy: $11.11
milk powder, 6.6 lb
butter, 4.4 lb
white cheese, salted, 2.2 lb
white cheese, unsalted, 2.2 lb
Italian cheese, sliced, 1.1 lb, not a weekly purchase
President cheese, 1 lb
yogurt, 8.8 oz

Meat, Fish, and Eggs: $33.22
farm chickens, 16.5 lb
lamb meat, 8.8 lb • Meat and meals are often shared
    with Nadia's brother, his wife, and their two small chil-
    dren—extended Egyptian families often live together,
    or close by, and eat together frequently, especially dur-
    ing holiday times.
eggs, 25
tuna, canned, 3 lb
beef burger patties, 1.1 lb
beef, frozen, 1.1 lb
Bordon corned beef, canned, 14 oz
meat, pickled, 8.8 oz

Fruits, Vegetables, and Nuts: $10.53
watermelons, 30.9 lb
yellow bananas, 5.5 lb
peaches, 4.4 lb
white eggplants, 7.7 lb
red onions, 6.6 lb
tomatoes, 6.6 lb
green olives, mixed with lemons, 4.4 lb
green bell peppers, 4.4 lb
squash, 4.4 lb
black olives, 2.2 lb
cucumbers, 2.2 lb
garlic, 2.2 lb
grape leaves, 2.2 lb
Jew's mallow (a traditional Egyptian vegetable used
    in soup), 2.2 lb
okra, 2.2 lb
beans, 1.1 lb
pickled vegetables, 1 qt

Condiments: $7.05
Yasmeena sunflower oil, 1.1 gal
sugar, 2.2 lb
Vigitar readymade filé spices, 1.8 lb
honey, 1.1 lb
coriander leaves (cilantro), 3 bunches
parsley, 3 bunches
black pepper, 7.9 oz
chile powder, 7.9 oz
coriander seed, 7.9 oz
cumin, 7.9 oz
mixed spices, powdered, 7.9 oz
salt, 7.1 oz, used as a seasoning, to salt pickles and to
    clean meat

Snacks: $1.33
halawa (sweet sesame cake), 2.2 lb

Prepared Food: $0.09
beans, cooked, 1 dish

Beverages: $2.47
Coca-Cola, 1.1 qt
Mirinda orange soda, 1.1 qt
Sprite, 1.1 qt
Al-Arousa tea, 1.1 lb
tap water for drinking and cooking

FACTS ABOUT EGYPT

Population of Cairo: 7,786,640

Population with access to electricity: 96%

Undernourished population: 3%

**Total annual health care expenditure per
    person in US$: $66**

Population age 20 and older with diabetes: 7.2%

**Consumption of sugar and sweeteners
    per person per year: 66 pounds**

Population living on less than $2 a day: 37%

**Camels imported into Egypt that are used for
    food: 90%**

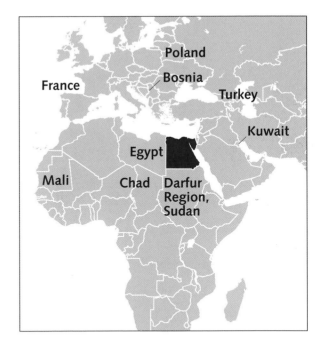

Nadia (left) and her sister-in-law Abadeer make *mahshi* (stuffed food, in this case small eggplants) on the floor of Nadia's fourth-floor apartment.

Muslims gather to pray at Al Fath Mosque (at right) in central Cairo.

There is nothing fast about Egyptian food, and on this steamy spring day in Cairo, it's probably just as well. Nadia Mohamed Ahmed and her sister-in-law Abadeer sit barefoot and cross-legged on the floor of Nadia's apartment, companionably coring baby eggplants and stuffing them with spicy chopped lamb for the evening meal. Eight-month-old Nancy calmly straddles one of her mother's shoulders, with one arm wrapped around Nadia's scarf-covered head. When the baby gets tired, Nadia slides her down from her perch and breastfeeds her but never stops stuffing. Nancy soon falls asleep and is tumbled onto a nearby bed adjacent to the kitchen, her arms outstretched, surrounded by pots and pans and food. The two mothers are unfazed by the noise of their other children, who are playing on the small, laundry-filled balcony overlooking a narrow street.

Gold bracelets tinkling, the women finish preparing the eggplant

and begin wrapping steamed grape leaves around a lemony mixture of rice, garlic, and lamb—stacking the tiny packages on a plate and talking all the while. The dishes are *mahshi,* which in Arabic means "stuffed."

Nadia's daughter Donya, fourteen, sits down to help them. Donya does not yet cover her hair with a scarf, but Nadia and Abadeer live as many women do in traditional Muslim cultures—mostly staying home, their hair covered in the presence of visitors, their husbands

A teenage boy delivers bread.

Nadia Ahmed's Okra Tagin with Mutton

30 cloves garlic, finely chopped
5 tablespoons corn oil
1 to 1½ pounds mutton, chopped
12 bay leaves
7 teaspoons cardamom seeds, ground
2 tablespoons black pepper
½ pound onion, finely chopped
2 pounds fresh tomato puree
2 pounds small green okra
4 ounces meat stock
2 tablespoons salt

Preheat the oven to 350°F.

Sauté the garlic in 1 tablespoon of the oil over medium heat until golden brown. Set aside.

In a stockpot, barely cover the meat with water, add the bay leaves, cardamom, and black pepper; bring to a low boil and simmer for 45 minutes.

Heat the remaining corn oil in a large frying pan over medium heat until hot, then fry the onion until it becomes translucent. Add the tomato puree, bring the mixture to a simmer, then add the okra and cook until soft, stirring frequently.

Add the stock to the meat mixture, and then combine with the okra mixture. Cook together over medium heat for 10 minutes.

Pour the mixture into a *tagin* (unglazed pottery-fired red clay pot) and stir in the sautéed garlic and salt. Put the tagin in the oven for 10 to 20 minutes, until tender.

managing their contact with the outside world. In a year's time, Donya too will cover her hair. Abadeer's husband, Rabie, enters the apartment, flops into a chair, and announces "My back hurts, and my knee." He's a tour guide in old Cairo and spends much of his time on the streets, trying to get hired. As he talks, he beckons to Abadeer with a flip of his hand; she jumps up to fetch him a glass of water, which he sips as she returns to work.

The two families live a floor apart in a crumbling old building above Islamic Cairo. This blend of medieval and modern life—buses and donkey carts, new cars and boys hauling goods, women covered and not—is unified by the call to prayer that issues from mosques throughout the city five times a day.

Nadia and Abadeer sit barefoot and crosslegged on the floor of Nadia's apartment, companionably coring baby eggplants and stuffing them with spicy chopped lamb for the evening meal.

France THE LE MOINES OF MONTREUIL

The Le Moine family in the living room of their apartment in the Paris suburb of Montreuil, with a week's worth of food. Michel Le Moine, 50, and Eve Le Moine, 50, stand behind their daughters, Delphine, 20 (standing), and Laetitia, 16 (holding spaghetti and Coppelius the cat). Cooking methods: electric stove, microwave oven. Food preservation: refrigerator-freezer. Favorite foods—Eve: fresh vegetables; Delphine: Thai food; Laetitia: pasta carbonara.

ONE WEEK'S FOOD IN NOVEMBER: 315.17 EUROS/$419.95 USD

Grains and Other Starchy Foods: $23.41
bread, 3.9 lb
English white bread, 1.8 lb
Barilla spaghetti, 1.1 lb
country bread, 1.1 lb
potatoes, 1.1 lb
croissants, with chocolate, 8.8 oz
Kellogg's corn flakes, 7.9 oz
croissants, 3.5 oz

Dairy: $24.45
Auchan (store brand) milk, 2.1 qt
Danone fruit yogurt, 2.2 lb
Yoplait Perle de Lait natural (plain) yogurt, 2.2 lb
chocolate yogurt, 1.3 lb
Yoplait Perle de Lait coconut yogurt, 1.1 lb
butter, 8.8 oz
Saint Nectaire cheese, 8.1 oz
goat cheese, 4.9 oz
Auchan Swiss cheese, grated, 2.5 oz

Meat, Fish, and Eggs: $92.29
beef, frozen, 2.2 lb
grenadier fish, 1.7 lb
salmon, 1.3 lb
eggs, 8
beef carpaccio, 1.2 lb
shrimp, 14.5 oz
chicken, 14.3 oz
Auchan sausage, 14.1 oz
Auchan ham, 12.7 oz
lamb, 12.3 oz
duck, 10.6 oz
rib eye steak, 7.4 oz
Auchan ham, sliced, 7.1 oz
tuna, 4.6 oz

Fruits, Vegetables, and Nuts: $54.96
pineapple, 2.9 lb
yellow bananas, 2.2 lb
persimmons, 2 lb
Royal Gala apples, 1.8 lb
pears, 1.1 lb
kiwis, 14.1 oz
oranges, 9.6 oz
prunes, 8.8 oz
green grapes, 7 oz
tangerines, 6.4 oz

mixed vegetables, fresh, 5.3 lb
mixed vegetables, frozen, 4.4 lb
tomatoes, 3.5 lb
pumpkin, 1.9 lb
hearts of palm, 1.8 lb
green beans, 15.5 oz
beetroot, 9.4 oz
cabbage, 8.8 oz
avocado, 1
artichokes, 6.9 oz
soy germ, 6.4 oz
scallions, 3.2 oz
Auchan chives, 1 bunch
garlic, 0.4 oz
walnuts, 1.1 lb

Condiments: $32.22
Maille vinegar, 1.3 qt
black currant jam, 10.6 oz
olive oil,‡ 10.2 fl oz
sunflower oil, 10.2 fl oz
honey, 7.1 oz
Nutella chocolate spread, 7.1 oz
ketchup, 6.2 oz
sugar, 5.3 oz
cornichons (small tart pickles), 3.5 oz
mayonnaise, 1.8 oz
mustard, 1.8 oz
parsley, 1 small bunch
basil,* 1 bunch
salt, 0.7 oz
celery salt, 0.5 oz
black basil, dried, 0.4 oz
black pepper, 0.1 oz

Snacks and Desserts: $17.10
apple compote (a dessert of stewed or baked fruit), 1.7 lb
Nestlé chocolate mousse, 12.7 oz
Gerblé orange soya biscuits, 9.9 oz
Nestlé raisin, hazelnut, almond dark chocolate, 8.8 oz
Balisto cereal bars, 7.1 oz
biscuits, 5.3 oz
Lindt dark chocolate, 3.5 oz
Nestlé caramel dark chocolate, 3.5 oz

Prepared Food: $85.66
tomato tabouleh, 1.2 lb
ham and mozzarella pizza, 15.9 oz
stuffed vine leaves, 14.1 oz

Auchan salad, 11.5 oz
surimi (Japanese frozen minced fish mixed with sugar and other additives), 7.1 oz
cafeteria food, 10 meals, with meat, vegetables, fruit, and bread

Fast Food: $32.51
Shanghai Express: sushi, 1 order
Chinese food, 1 order
McDonald's: 1 McChicken sandwich, French fries, *Evian* water.

Beverages: $44.76
Wattwiller mineral water, 2 gal
Vernière mineral water, 2 gal
Volvic mineral water, 3.2 qt
orange juice, 2 1.1-qt cartons
Sojasun soy milk, 2 1.1-qt cartons
Auchan tomato juice, 1.1 qt
Joker carrot juice, 1.1 qt
Tropicana fruit juice, 1.1 qt
cider, 25.4 fl oz
red wine, 25.4 fl oz
William Grant's whiskey, 5 fl oz
Auchan coffee, 2.5 oz
Twinings of London Earl Grey tea, 25 teabags

Miscellaneous: $12.59
Auchan assorted cat food, 3.5 lb
Friskies cat food, 15.9 oz.

*Homegrown
‡ Not in photo

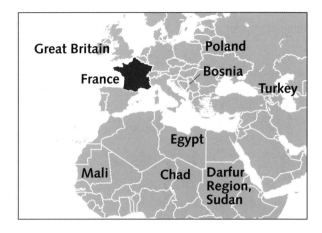

When twenty-year-old Delphine Le Moine hosts a weekend dinner party for friends, she serves traditional French gratins and subtle meat dishes, meals complete with cheese and salad courses, rich desserts, and bottles of French wine. But when her family sits down for a weeknight dinner, the fare is more global in nature and more convenience-oriented.

Although Delphine's parents, Michel and Eve, grieve about how neighborhood groceries are closing because they can't compete with the big chains, they themselves usually opt for the low prices and the convenience of shopping at the French supermarket Auchan. "There are still the classic French shops, the patisseries, *boulangeries,* butcher shops, greengrocers, and cheese shops where we can buy better-quality food than in the supermarkets," says Michel, a software engineer and lover of gourmet food, "but at higher prices." The Le Moines, who live just outside Paris, are not alone, and because of the trend toward supermarkets, the specialty shops that once defined France are disappearing.

Immigrants to France—nearly one in four Parisians is foreign-born—have introduced a wide variety of foods to the country. Michel

"It's very pleasant to taste food from other countries. However, I think too many young people eat American food, and I am a bit afraid that French food will disappear in a few years." But when Delphine is pressed for time, she too ducks into the nearest McDonald's.

During the family's weekly shopping trip to the huge Auchan supersized supermarket, Delphine prints a price tag for her tomatoes at a produce-weighing station.

loves the broadening of the French palate, but he dislikes what he sees as the changing nature of the table as a gathering place. "Young people spend less and less time eating," he says. "They only feed—they don't really appreciate mealtimes."

His daughters, caught up in their increasingly frenzied lives, are part of this new French style of eating. During the school week, Delphine, who attends a dance academy in Paris, and her sister, Laetitia, sixteen, a high school student, lunch mostly on yogurt, Chinese takeout, and other fast food.

Delphine voices another concern: "It's very pleasant to taste food from other countries. However, I think too many young people eat American food, and I am a bit afraid that French food will disappear in a few years." But when she's pressed for time, she too ducks into the nearest McDonald's. When the girls were younger, they ate their lunches in the school cafeteria. Workplace and school cafeterias in France are closer to fine restaurant dining than cafeterias, as Americans know them. On a scale of one to ten, the parents rate cafeteria fare as an eight or nine in both nutrition and taste.

Michel, whose mother created meals from the bounty of their neighborhood greengrocer, says that making good choices from among the many new options is the key: "I am convinced that the food we eat now is as healthy as before, and maybe healthier, although we buy already prepared salads, and we open packages and the food is ready." Eve grew up in the countryside, in a home with no refrigerator; her mother made food purchases daily and had a garden overflowing with vegetables. For now, though, Eve can only savor the memories. Her refrigerator is full, but so is her schedule. Often, the fine French meal has to wait.

Delphine Le Moine, a dance major (above center), stretches before her class at the Centre International de Danse Jazz Rick Odums.

After the family food portrait, the Le Moines (left) gamely tried to use up as much of the perishable food as possible in that night's supper.

Great Britain THE BAINTONS OF COLLINGBOURNE DUCIS

The Bainton family in the dining area of their living room in Collingbourne Ducis, Wiltshire, with a week's worth of food. Left to right: Mark Bainton, 44, Deb Bainton, 45 (petting Polo the dog), and sons Josh, 14, and Tadd, 12. Cooking methods: electric stove, microwave oven. Food preservation: refrigerator-freezer, a second small freezer. Favorite foods—Mark: avocado; Deb: prawn-mayonnaise sandwich; Josh: prawn cocktail; Tadd: chocolate fudge cake with cream.

ONE WEEK'S FOOD IN NOVEMBER: 155.54 BRITISH POUNDS/$253.15 USD

Grains and Other Starchy Foods: $20.41
white potatoes, 3.9 lb; new (young) potatoes, 1.3 lb
Kingsmill Gold soft white bread, sliced, 2 loaves
Hovis crusty white bread, 1.8 lb
Weetabix whole grain cereal, 1.5 lb
McDougall's self-raising flour, 1.1 lb
Saxby puff pastry, 1.1 lb
Seeds of Change tagliatelle, 1.1 lb
Waitrose (store brand) porridge oats, 1.1 lb
Kellogg's Coco Pops, 13 oz
Waitrose corn flakes, 12 oz
Waitrose garlic baguette, organic, 6 oz
Jacob's TUC crackers, 5.3 oz

Dairy: $27.93
semi-skim milk, 3.5 gal
full-cream milk (whole), 2 qt
Waitrose strawberry yogurt, 1.5 lb
Müller Corner strawberry yogurt, 1.2 lb
Waitrose custard, 1.1 lb
mild English Cheddar, 11.5 oz
Philadelphia cream cheese, 8 oz
Waitrose rhubarb yogurt and toffee yogurt, 6 oz each
Country Life butter, 4.4 oz
Cropwell Bishop cheese, 3.5 oz

Meat, Fish, and Eggs: $28.34
Waitrose British pork, 2.2 lb
Waitrose eggs, 12
Waitrose pork escalopes,‡ 1.1 lb
Waitrose tuna, canned in brine, 1.1 lb
honey-roasted ham, 11.8 oz
Waitrose unsmoked British bacon, 5.5 oz
Waitrose large prawns, frozen, 5.3 oz

Fruits, Vegetables, and Nuts: $35.27
Coxes variety apples, 2.8 lb
Braeburn variety apples, 1.8 lb
yellow bananas, 1.5 lb
oranges, 1.4 lb
Granny Smith variety apples, 1.3 lb
green grapes, seedless, 14.4 oz
Del Monte pineapple chunks, canned, 8 oz
Heinz baked beans, canned, 2.8 lb
Waitrose brussel sprouts, fresh, 2.2 lb
Birds Eye garden peas, frozen, 2 lb
white cabbage, organic, 1 head
white mushrooms, 1.6 lb

cauliflower, 1 head
carrots, 1.5 lb
parsnips, 1.2 lb
iceberg lettuce, 1 head
tomatoes, 1 lb
broccoli, 13.9 oz
cucumber, 11.2 oz
red onion, 10.6 oz
runner beans, 10.2 oz
mange-tout peas (snow peas), 5.3 oz
sugar snap peas, 5.3 oz

Condiments: $20.34
I Can't Believe It's Not Butter spread, 15 oz
Heinz ketchup, 14 oz
Hartley's Best raspberry jam, 12 oz
Heinz salad cream, 10 oz
Hellmann's Real mayonnaise, 10 oz
Waitrose smooth peanut butter, organic, 8 oz
Waitrose blend olive oil, 5.1 fl oz
Tate Lyle white sugar, 4.4 oz
Waitrose dark-brown muscovado sugar, 3.5 oz
Waldorf salad topping, 1.8 oz
paprika, 1.7 oz
black pepper, 1.4 oz
Maldon sea salt, *Saxa* table salt, 1 oz each
basil,* parsley,* 1 bunch each
Sweetex sweetener, 80 tablets (these are very small)

Snacks and Desserts: $28.74
McCain oven chips (French fries), frozen, 2 lb
Mars candy bars, multipacks, 1.7 lb
Waitrose savory wedges,‡ frozen, 1.7 lb
Waitrose milk chocolate digestive biscuits, 14.1 oz
Waitrose treacle tart, 13.4 oz
Cadbury twirls, 8.9 oz
Trebor Softmints, 7.9 oz
Haribo Maoam Stripes, 7.1 oz
Waitrose rich tea biscuits, 7.1 oz
Golden Wonder Nik Naks, 6.6 oz
Walker's BBQ crisps, 6.2 oz
Walker's prawn cocktail crisps, 6.2 oz
Waitrose caramel surprise, 5.3 oz
Waitrose chocolate surprise, 5.3 oz
Onken chocolate & hazelnut mousse, 4.4 oz
strawberry laces, 3.5 oz
Waitrose mini jelly babies, 3.5 oz
Dairylea Double Dunker nachos, 1.8 oz
Flying Saucers candy, 1.8 oz

Prepared Food: $26.01
New Covent Garden Food Co vegetable and lentil
    soup, 1.3 lb
Waitrose five-cheese and pepperoni pizza, 1.3 lb
Loyd Grossman four-cheese pasta sauce, 15.9 oz
Heinz cream of tomato soup, canned, 14.1 oz
Waitrose cheese and onion flan, 14.1 oz
Waitrose chicken and mushroom flan, 14.1 oz
Dairylea ham Lunchables, 7.8 oz
Bisto granules gravy mix, roast vegetable flavored, 7.1 oz
Waitrose carbonara sauce, 5.3 oz

Homemade Food:
savory pancakes, made with flour, milk, and eggs (above)

Beverages: $38.51
Capri Sun fruit juice, 12 6.8-fl-oz packages
Somerfield Pennine Valley water, 1.6 qt
Wadworth beer, 12 16.9-fl-oz cans
Waitrose pineapple juice, press apple juice, and pure
    orange juice, 1.1 qt each
Tesco mountain spring water, 16.9 fl oz
Cadbury drinking chocolate, 1.1 lb
James Herrick red wine, 12.7 fl oz
Douwe Egberts Continental Gold coffee, 6.2 oz
PG Tips tea, 40 teabags
tap water, for drinking and cooking

Miscellaneous: $27.60
Waitrose variety cat food, 5.4 lb
Bakers dog food, rabbit and vegetable, dry 3.3 lb
Pedigree dog food, chicken and game, canned, 1.8 lb
Friskies Go-Cat cat food, dry, 13.2 oz
Golden Virginia hand-rolling tobacco, 3.5 oz
Rizla cigarette papers, 4 packs

*Homegrown
‡Not in photo

On the weekends, there's cooked breakfast, but during the week, cold cereal for breakfast is routine.

D eb Bainton calls her son Josh an "almost vegetarian." She says, half jokingly, that any day now a hearty lentil soup will replace the traditional British Sunday roast. "But I do like a roast," says her husband, Mark, with comic wistfulness.

There is actually no danger that he might miss out on this. "We're often eating different meals at the same table," says Deb.

"We're having a proper English cooked breakfast this morning—eggs, bacon, mushrooms, and stewed tomato," says Deb. While sons Josh, fourteen, and Tadd, twelve, focus on Saturday morning cartoons, Mark mans the skillet, with Deb as assistant. When both egg and eggshell land in the sputtering grease, Deb says amiably, "Roughage." As she picks out the eggshell, Josh decides to have cold cereal instead.

This weekend the Baintons and some of Josh's friends will celebrate his fourteenth birthday at the local pub, with dinner, a cake, a spray can of whipped cream, and a game of pool. But first, it's time for the weekly food shopping—no one's favorite chore. They hop in the car and drive through their quaint little village, Collingbourne

PHOTOGRAPHER'S FIELD NOTE

I was excited about going to the Baintons' house in southwest England because they live near the mysterious stone circles of Stonehenge, which I had never seen before. Since Stonehenge is open only from 9:30 A.M. until 4:00 P.M. and is surrounded by fences, you can't get anywhere near it for photographs at dawn or sunset, when the light is best. Getting up at 4:00 A.M., I drove through the swirling mist in the dark past Stonehenge, pulled into a pasture, and crept through the fields toward the site. The police were onto me within a hundred yards. I flashed my press card but they were in no mood to make post-9/11 exceptions. Actually, they were pretty nice not to arrest me, especially when I told them that the real mystery of Stonehenge is why it is not open at interesting hours.

Ducis, named in part for a long-dead duke. They take pastoral byways, past quaint thatched cottages, cow crossings, and military tank crossing signs, through half a dozen other equally quaint little villages in Wiltshire, until the modern world swings briskly into view in the form of Waitrose, the upscale U.K. grocery chain in the town of Marlborough. Mark grabs a shopping cart and they head inside.

"I push the trolley," says Mark, "but I'm banned from shopping." "All sorts of strange foods end up in our cupboards when Mark does the food shop," says Deb, "and he buys lots of sweets." The boys, and Deb, too, are no strangers to sweet things, although Josh's favorite item to sneak into the trolley is very expensive prawns (shrimp). They stock up on convenience foods like frozen pizza and juice-boxes to get them through the week.

Friends and family celebrate Josh Bainton's fourteenth birthday party on Saturday night at The Crown, the neighborhood pub.

STREET FOOD

Street food is generally cheap and fast: Chinese teenagers choose a skewer of deep-fried scorpions; Middle Eastern vendors sell spicy kebabs and *shwarma*, and glasses of tea are carried overhead on trays from teashops to local businessmen. For vendors, the street is a cheap place to cook, especially in cities like Manila, where unemployment is very high, and Mexico City, where cooks toss together spicy tacos on corn tortillas. For foreign visitors, the tastes of the street are an introduction to a new culture. For locals, it's the original fast food.

Cotton candy • Cairo, Egypt

Hot pretzels near the blue mosque • Istanbul, Turkey

Chicken vendors • Phnom Penh, Cambodia

Sea horses, cicadas, silkworm pupae • Beijing, China

Pineapple and mango chunks • Colombo, Sri Lanka

Pig and chicken intestines, fatty pork • Manila, Philippines

Red salty eggs • Manila, Philippines

Sheep's head soup • Zumbagua, Ecuador

Spit-roasted *cuy* (guinea pig) • Ambato, Ecuador

Betel nut vendor • Varanasi, India

ANNUAL MEAT CONSUMPTION

COUNTRY	🐔 = roughly 10 pounds of meat (poultry, pig, bovine, goat, and sheep)	per person, in pounds
Australia	🐔🐔🐔🐔🐔🐔🐔🐔🐔🐔🐔🐔🐔🐔🐔🐔🐔🐔🐔🐔🐔🐔🐔🐔	247
Bhutan*	🐔	7
Bosnia and Herzegovina	🐔🐔🐔🐔	43
Chad	🐔🐔🐔	33
China	🐔🐔🐔🐔🐔🐔🐔🐔🐔🐔🐔🐔	117
Darfun Region, Sudan	N/A	N/A
Ecuador	🐔🐔🐔🐔🐔🐔🐔🐔🐔🐔	96
Egypt	🐔🐔🐔🐔🐔	45
France	🐔🐔🐔🐔🐔🐔🐔🐔🐔🐔🐔🐔🐔🐔🐔🐔🐔🐔🐔🐔🐔🐔	219
Great Britain	🐔🐔🐔🐔🐔🐔🐔🐔🐔🐔🐔🐔🐔🐔🐔🐔🐔🐔	179
Greenland*	🐔🐔🐔🐔🐔🐔🐔🐔🐔🐔🐔🐔🐔🐔🐔🐔🐔🐔🐔🐔🐔🐔🐔🐔🐔	250
Guatemala	🐔🐔🐔🐔🐔	51
India	🐔	11
Japan	🐔🐔🐔🐔🐔🐔🐔🐔🐔🐔	95
Kuwait	🐔🐔🐔🐔🐔🐔🐔🐔🐔🐔🐔🐔🐔🐔	142
Mali	🐔🐔🐔🐔	40
Mexico	🐔🐔🐔🐔🐔🐔🐔🐔🐔🐔🐔🐔🐔	128
Mongolia	🐔🐔🐔🐔🐔🐔🐔🐔🐔🐔🐔🐔🐔🐔🐔🐔🐔🐔🐔🐔🐔	215
Philippines	🐔🐔🐔🐔🐔🐔🐔	66
Poland	🐔🐔🐔🐔🐔🐔🐔🐔🐔🐔🐔🐔🐔🐔🐔🐔	161
Turkey	🐔🐔🐔🐔	44
United States	🐔🐔🐔🐔🐔🐔🐔🐔🐔🐔🐔🐔🐔🐔🐔🐔🐔🐔🐔🐔🐔🐔🐔🐔🐔🐔🐔	270

Source: Food and Agriculture Organization of the United Nations (2001–3)

*Bhutan and Greenland source: World Resources Institute, Earth Trends (2002)

N/A = Information not available

AVAILABLE DAILY CALORIC INTAKE

Snacking on small potatoes and corn • Ecuador

Distributing bags of corn-soy mixture and sorghum • Chad

COUNTRY	calories per person, per day
Australia	3,120
Bhutan	N/A
Bosnia and Herzegovina	2,730
Chad	2,130
China	2,930
Darfur Region, Sudan	N/A
Ecuador	2,670
Egypt	3,330
France	3,630
Great Britain	3,460
Greenland	N/A
Guatemala	2,230
India	2,470
Japan	2,270
Kuwait	3,110
Mali	2,200
Mexico	3,170
Mongolia	2,250
Philippines	2,490
Poland	3,420
Turkey	3,320
United States	3,760

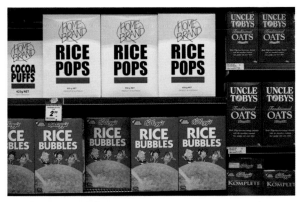

Local variations of American Rice Crispies • Australia

Sampling daikon at a public market • Japan

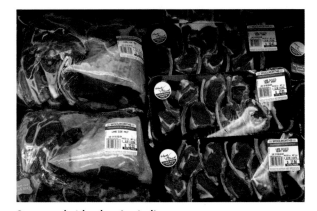

Supermarket lamb • Australia

Source: Food and Agriculture Organization of the UN (2002–4)
N/A = Information not available

Greenland THE MADSENS OF CAP HOPE

The Madsen family in their living room in Cap Hope village, Greenland, with a week's worth of food. Standing by the TV are Emil Madsen, 40, and Erika Madsen, 26, with their children (left to right) Martin, 9, Belissa, 6, and Abraham, 12. Cooking method: gas stove. Food preservation: refrigerator-freezer. Favorite foods—Emil: polar bear; Erika: narwhal skin; Abraham and Belissa: Greenlandic food; Martin: Danish food.

ONE WEEK'S FOOD IN MAY: 1,928.80 DANISH KRONE/$277.04 USD

Grains and Other Starchy Foods: $34.07
brown bread, 2 loaves
High Class white rice, 2.2 lb
Ota sol gryn (muesli-like cereal), 2.1 lb
Finax fruit muesli, 1.7 lb
hard biscuits, 1.5 lb, tucked into pockets for quick snacks
hard bread, 1 loaf
Bellaroma farfalle, 1.1 lb
Bellaroma fusilli, 1.1 lb
Foodline rice, 1.1 lb
Quaker Oats Guldkorn (corn cereal), 1.1 lb
Foodline mashed potato mix, 15.5 oz
Dagens white bread rolls, frozen, 12

Dairy: $4.87
Arinco milk, powdered, 4.4 lb, makes 1.9 gal
Lurpak butter, 13.2 oz.

Meat, Fish, and Eggs: $53.97**
musk ox,* 26.5 lb
walrus,* frozen, 9.9 lb
arctic geese,* 8.8 lb meat, after cleaning
polar bear,* 3.3 lb
Tulip hot dogs, 3 lb
little auk (also called dovekie),* 5 birds, 1.9 lb
ground beef, frozen, 1.7 lb
Danish sausage, frozen, 1.1 lb
ham, 1.1 lb
Danish Prime meatballs, frozen, 14.1 oz
cod, dried, 12.4 oz, eaten with narwhal oil
breakfast meat and 4 slices of egg, 10.6 oz, egg product
  purchased in tube form called "long egg"
Danish Prime Danish meatballs, frozen, 8.5 oz
capelin (fish), 7.8 oz
Tulip bacon, 5.3 oz

Fruits, Vegetables, and Nuts: $8.67
Nycol oranges, canned, 1.4 lb
Sunsiesta fruit cocktail, canned, 11 oz
yellow onions, 1.3 lb
Bellaroma tomato sauce, chili pepper flavored, 14.1 oz
Frontline champignon mushrooms, preserved, 9.9 oz

Condiments: $25.66
Heinz tomato ketchup, 3.2 lb
Jozo salt, 2.2 lb
Dan Sukker sugar, 1.1 lb
narwhal oil, approx. 16 fl oz, varying amounts depending
  on whether anyone has shot one recently
HP sauce, 15 oz
marmalade, 14.1 oz
Foodline chocolate cream, 12.4 oz
coffee creamer, powdered, 10.6 oz
Lea & Perrins Worcestershire sauce, 8.5 fl oz
K mayonnaise, 7.1 oz
K remoulade, 7.1 oz
Foodline onions, dried, 1.8 oz
black pepper, 1.1 oz

Snacks and Desserts: $54.25
candy, assorted, 3.3 lb
Haribo Maoam mini fruit candies, 11.6 oz
Marabou chocolate bar, 10.2 oz
KiMs X-tra potato crisps, 8.8 oz
Pringles Original potato chips, 8.8 oz
raisins, 8.8 oz
LU Ritz crackers, 7.1 oz
Göteborgs ballerina cookies, 6.4 oz
LU mini TUC (crackers), 5.3 oz
Milky Way candy bars, 4.1 oz
Bisca Chocolate Marie cookies, 3.5 oz
bubble mix chewing gum, 3.5 oz
Mamba candy, 2.7 oz
Bounty candy bar, 2 oz
Stimorol chewing gum, 1 pack

Prepared Food: $35.66
Knorr chicken bouillon, 2.5 lb
Nissin cup noodles, instant, 2.3 lb
Daloon spring rolls, frozen, 1.9 lb
Danish Prime sausage mix (sausage and potato),
  frozen, 1.3 lb
Knorr Mexican dried soup base, 10.6 oz
Knorr minestrone dried soup base, 10.6 oz
liver paste, 7.1 oz

Beverages: $36.40
mixed fruit drink concentrate, 3.2 qt
orange drink concentrate, 3.2 qt
Rynkeby apple juice, 2.1 qt
Rynkeby orange juice, 1.1 qt
Coca-Cola, 12 fl oz
Faxe Kondi (carbonated drink), 12 fl oz
Nikoline lemon (carbonated drink), 12 fl oz
Nikoline orange (carbonated drink), 12 fl oz
7UP, 12 fl oz
Nescafé instant coffee, 10.6 oz
Pickwick lemon tea, 20 teabags
Pickwick tropical fruit tea, 20 teabags
spring water, in milk cans, used for drinking and cooking

Miscellaneous: $23.49
Prince cigarettes, 3 packs

*Hunted
**Local value of hunted meat: $221.26

Hunter Emil Madsen stops briefly in the town of Ittoqqortoormiit, on Greenland's central east coast, after a five-day hunting trip. The Greenlander, of Inuit descent, is there to buy groceries—his tiny village of Cap Hope, two hours away by dogsled, has no market, only a small government shop that sells nonperishable foods. There are no roads to Ittoqqortoormiit—Ittoq, as the locals call it—and the next large settlement is five hundred miles away. Provisions come to Ittoq by boat during the summer and by air or snowmobile, over frozen Scoresby Sound, during the rest of the year.

To break the monotony of dogsled travel, 9-year-old Martin runs alongside.

Afterward, we pile onto his dog sled for the long drive to his home. Emil barks commands in Greenlandic to the fourteen dogs in his team, starting their trek west, along the Sound, past towering icebergs and frosted mountains, and endless snow. We skim across the snow for well over two hours, bumping over old sled tracks and dog poop—a trip that would take eight or ten minutes in a car . . . if there were a road.

Emil's youngest child, Belissa, a round-faced girl with an ear-to-ear smile, greets her father with a hug at the door of their modern clapboard house in Cap Hope. Throughout the evening, the four children horse around, dividing their attention between MTV and Emil's conversations with his fellow hunters who trickle in for midnight musk ox stew.

At breakfast time the next day, there's lots of tea, juice from a sugary fruit concentrate, and muesli in reconstituted powdered milk, accompanied by Danish dance videos and more MTV. Meals are prepared in the family's small modern kitchen, which has all the usual amenities except running water, and are eaten in front of the television—whether or not there are guests. No one is in a hurry to get going because at this time of year there's continuous daylight. After breakfast, Erika passes supplies for a family camping trip through an open window to sons Abraham and Martin: a hunk of frozen musk ox meat in a plastic bag; a weather-tight bin full of packaged noodles, cookies, and muesli; a soup pot; ice pikes for fishing; and a portable kerosene cook stove. The boys pile everything onto one of the two dogsleds.

It's May, a comparatively warm month, when the temperature hovers around freezing. Erika says she doesn't feel the cold; she grew up with it. On the second sled, the two boys keep warm by jumping on and off the sled and racing next to it. After hours of travel, Emil and Erika make a campsite on an inland glacial lake. Meanwhile, the boys punch fishing holes through the lake's four-foot-thick ice with long, spearlike pikes. Snow-white hares bound across the ice in the

A wooden cross stands guard over the village cemetery in Cap Hope. Now home to just ten people, Cap Hope is where both Emil and Erika Madsen grew up. During the summer at Cap Hope, the sun never actually disappears below the horizon, though it does dip briefly behind the high hills that surround the village.

distance as Erika, Emil, and the children fish companionably until 2 A.M., and then drop the catch in the snow outside the tent in the bright light of bedtime. Normally they would be in school this time of year, but their school schedule is set by their teacher, who is also their grandmother. She's paid by the government to teach classes in their small village. The Madsens are her only pupils and therefore the schedule is more flexible than most.

The next day the fishing continues, with the pile of char growing to at least one hundred. Erika cleans the fish, and Emil steams a bunch of them in a pot of melted snow. Then it's off again on the sleds: Emil is going to hunt for seal.

At the ice edge, the family concentrates on the open water, looking for a seal that recently popped its head up. Everyone is silent as they get off the sleds. Abraham sets down the wooden gun rest, and Emil lies on the snow with his rifle. A small shiny head breaks the water's surface briefly, and Emil takes a shot. He hits the seal but can't tell whether he's killed or wounded it. Meanwhile, the rest of the family drags the skiff—there's one on the second sled—into the

Greenlandic Seal Stew

2 pounds seal meat, chunked
2 ounces rice
Salt
1 onion, sliced thick

Put meat and rice in a pot, add water to cover, and bring to a boil over high heat. Add salt to taste and onion. Boil for 45 minutes to 1 hour, until meat is tender.

At breakfast, Emil's 10-year-old nephew Julian, who is visiting for a week, plays air guitar and eats sugar-drenched muesli while watching MTV in the Madsens' living room with his cousin Belissa (left).

After a five-hour sled ride from Cap Hope, everyone wolfs down Emil's musk ox stew with pasta in the canvas tent (above). The next day Erika yanks char out of the hole with a practiced motion (above left).

While Emil stows away the gear and winches the boat ashore, nephew Julian and son Abraham drag the freshly killed seal up to the house (opposite).

water. Emil jumps into the boat and rows furiously toward the spot where blood is burbling to the surface; meanwhile Erika and the boys shovel-cut an angled ramp into the ice edge to pull up the boat when he returns. Everyone watches as Emil stops the skiff by the blood and waits, rifle at the ready, one hundred feet offshore. The wounded seal has disappeared. Thwarted, Emil returns and is pulled up the ramp. Such failures don't happen very often. Last year, Emil killed a polar bear, some walrus, musk ox, a few narwhals, many seabirds and hares—and 175 seals. The family and their friends ate the meat,

the dogs ate the entrails and bones, and the Madsens either sold the skins or used them themselves.

Although the miss discourages him, Emil doesn't give up. He has a speedboat in Cap Hope (these replaced traditional kayaks long ago). After the two-hour mush home, he heads out to try again. A V-shaped ripple in the water draws Emil's attention. He slows to a gentle stop, then shoots the seal, killing it with one shot. Julian helps him drag the animal onto the back of the boat. They head home, where Erika will butcher the seal in the morning.

Guatemala THE MENDOZAS OF TODOS SANTOS

The Mendoza family and a servant in their courtyard in Todos Santos Cuchumatán, Guatemala, with a week's worth of food. Between Fortunato Pablo Mendoza, 50, and Susana Mendoza, 47, stand (left to right) Ignacio, 15, Cristolina, 19, and a family friend (standing in for daughter Marcelucia, 9, who ran off to play). Far right: Sandra Ramos, 11, live-in helper. Not present: Xtila, 17, and Juan, 12. Cooking methods: gas stovetop, wood stove. Food preservation: refrigerator.

ONE WEEK'S FOOD IN NOVEMBER: 573 QUETZALES/$75.70 USD

Grains and Other Starchy Foods: $11.49**
corn (yellow and white mixed),* 48 lb
potatoes, 20 lb
masa (corn tortilla dough), 8 lb
Inti pasta, 4.4 lb
corn tortillas, 4 lb
Quaker Avena Mosh (oat breakfast cereal), 1.1 lb
rice,‡ 1 lb

Dairy: $2.25
milk, powdered, 14.1 oz

Meat, Fish, and Eggs: $7.93
chickens, 4.4 lb • Two other chickens in the photograph
    are for the All Saints Day celebration.
eggs, 30

Fruits, Vegetables, and Nuts: $34.75
yellow bananas, 7.4 lb
pineapples, 6.4 lb
zapote (brown-colored fruit), 5 lb
passion fruit, 3.9 lb
anona (custard apples), 3.2 lb
oranges, 2.6 lb
lemons, 2.2 lb
black beans, dried, 13.2 lb
green squash, 12 lb
tomatoes, 10 lb
carrots, 7.8 lb
avocados, 5 lb
white onions, 5 lb
cauliflower, 3 heads
green beans, 4.4 lb
cucumbers, 3.5 lb
chayote squash, 3.2 lb
green onions, 3 lb
cabbage, 1 head
red chile peppers, 1.5 lb
green chile peppers, 8.8 oz

Condiments: $8.85
oil, 3.2 qt
herbs, assorted, fresh, 1 bunch
white sugar, 5 oz
Malher black pepper, 3 oz
Malher garlic salt, 3 oz
Malher onion salt, 3 oz
Malher salt, 3 oz
cinnamon, 2 sticks

Snacks: $3.96
chocolate, hand-pressed, 1 lb
Azteca tortilla chips, 5 bags

Prepared Food: $0.79
Malher chicken bouillon, 3 oz

Beverages: $5.68
bottled water, 5 gal, for drinking only
Corazon de Trigo (wheat drink), 1.1 lb
Incasa coffee, 8 oz

*Homegrown
‡Not in photo
**Market value of homegrown foods, if purchased
    locally: $4.12

The Mendoza kitchen is the center of family life. "I am happiest," Fortunato says, "when I'm eating Susana's rice and beans, her homemade tortillas, and her turkey soup."

United States

Mexico

Guatemala

Ecuador

Especially busy during the days before the holidays, the village market spills out of the big concrete municipal market and extends down side streets.

Fortunato and Susana Mendoza's daughter Cristolina, nineteen, is the queen of the town festival this warm November day, but before she can celebrate she has to beat a rival team in basketball and help her mother cook dinner for a gathering of their family and friends. Today they're preparing turkey soup from the old turkey that used to peck at dried corn and insects outside their adobe house. Most families in Todos Santos eat meat less than once a week, except during holidays. Three times a day they eat rice, beans, potatoes, eggs, and tortillas, in one combination or another.

"We don't have fish, as we live so far from the sea," says Susana. Cristolina tells us that they don't eat candies and cakes. "If we want a *postre* (dessert), we have a banana," she says, her smile revealing beautifully white, cavity-free teeth. Although soft drinks are available in the village, and in fact the Mendozas sell them in their new bar, the family drinks only water, a wheat drink, and instant coffee.

The Mendozas eat fruits and vegetables only when they are in season because local stores don't have the refrigeration and transportation necessary to stock out-of-season items. Though potatoes are plentiful in the village, when Cristolina was studying in another part of Guatemala, five hours away, she didn't eat potatoes. "The price was incredible," she exclaims, "twice the cost of potatoes here, and very small." Did she miss eating potatoes? "Oh yes," she says.

The brightly decorated cemetery in the remote mountain town of Todos Santos Cuchumatán becomes brighter still as an artist from Guatemala City puts the final touches to a cross in multicolor splendor. Around him, women sweep and scrub their family plots for the celebration of *Dia de Todos Santos*—All Saints Day. Outside the burial ground, slaughtered sheep destined for the dinner table hang from the houses, and family members get together to help with the skinning and cutting or to give advice. This weekend is a double holiday for the Todosanteros, a celebration of both All Saints the Christian holiday and All Saints the village. Musicians with guitars and marimbas blend in with the villagers on their narrow streets and delight the tourists who mill about.

The villagers of Todos Santos are a hard-working lot, farmers who grow corn, beans, potatoes, wheat, barley, and sugar cane; many are indigenous Maya and still speak Mam, the Mayan language. As visitors from abroad have become more common, some townspeople have launched a side business, renting rooms in their small adobe houses to students from other countries who attend the little schools that have sprung up to teach Spanish. Women teach visitors intricate weaving on the backstrap loom, which has one end strapped around the weaver's waist; others run bars and restaurants.

Fortunato, a college-educated teacher, musician, renter of rooms, and shaman, is a bit of an oddity in this rural village; although skilled at navigating the wider world—he's managed to get his children into good colleges—he remains firmly rooted in his traditional culture. On any given night, Susana and Fortunato welcome the assortment of friends and relatives who invariably turn up at dinnertime for a good meal and conversations that can ramble long into the night.

FAMILY RECIPE

Susana's Turkey Soup

1 10-pound live turkey
5 pounds cornmeal
3 2-ounce packets ground pepper
4 chicken or vegetable bouillon cubes
Salt

Kill and dress the turkey (the turkey should be about 6 pounds dressed).

Cut the turkey meat into medium-size pieces. Rinse and put in a pot large enough to contain the meat with enough water to make soup for ten people. Simmer for 2 to 4 hours, until tender, then remove the meat, set aside, and reserve the broth.

In a separate bowl, beat the cornmeal with enough cold water to make a thick porridge, then add the cornmeal mixture to the broth and bring to a boil. Add the pepper, bouillon cubes, and salt to taste.

Add the meat back to the broth. Let boil for 6 minutes.

Throughout the town, many people have their own turkeys and sheep, which they slaughter for special family reunions during festival days.

India THE PATKARS OF UJJAIN

The Patkar family—Jayant, 48, Sangeeta, 42, daughter Neha, 19, and son Akshay, 15—in the living room of their home in Ujjain, Madhya Pradesh, India, with one week's worth of food. Cooking method: gas stove. Food preservation: refrigerator-freezer.

ONE WEEK'S FOOD IN APRIL: 1,636.25 RUPEES/$39.27 USD

Grains and Other Starchy Foods: $5.35
chapatis (flat bread), 13.2 lb
wheat flour, 8.8 lb
potatoes, 3.3 lb
white rice, 3.3 lb
poha (flattened white rice), 2.2 lb
Modern Special white bread, sliced, 1 loaf
wheat porridge, 1.1 lb
chickpea flour, 1.1 lb

Dairy: $9.70
milk,‡ 1.9 gal
yogurt curds, 4.4 lb
Nestlé Everyday Dairy Whitener milk powder, 1.1 lb
ice cream, assorted flavors, 15.9 oz
ghee (clarified butter), 8.8 oz

Meat, Fish, and Eggs:
Like most Hindus, the Patkar family does not eat meat
    or fish.

Fruits, Vegetables, and Nuts: $7.73
watermelon, 6.6 lb
oranges, 4.4 lb
green grapes, 2.2 lb
limes, 12.8 oz
coconut, one-half
red onions, 5.5 lb
gourd, 3.3 lb
bitter gourd, 2.2 lb
cabbage, 2 heads
cauliflower, 1 head
tomatoes, 2.2 lb
yellow lentils, 2.2 lb
eggplant, 1.7 lb
chickpeas, 1.1 lb
cucumber, 1.1 lb
green lentils, 1.1 lb
okra (also called lady fingers), 1.1 lb
red beans, 1.1 lb
black-eyed beans, 8.8 oz
coriander, 8.8 oz
green bell pepper, 8.8 oz
green chile peppers, 3.5 oz
ground nuts, 1.1 lb

Condiments: $4.47
soybean oil, 1.1 qt
salt, 1.1 lb
Nilon's pickles, 8.8 oz
white sugar, 8.8 oz
Maggi tomato ketchup, 7.1 oz
cumin seed, 3.5 oz
fenugreek seed, 3.5 oz
mint, 3.5 oz
mustard seed, 3.5 oz
black pepper, 1.8 oz
garlic chutney, 1.8 oz
mango, dried and powdered, 1.8 oz
parsley, 1.8 oz
red chile powder, 1.8 oz
aniseed, 0.9 oz
turmeric powder, 0.9 oz
asafetida (powdered gum resin), 0.4 oz
cloves, 0.4 oz

Snacks and Desserts: $2.33
gulab jamoon (deep-fried dumplings), 1.1 lb, served
    soaked in cardamom-flavored syrup
upma rawa (savory semolina dish), 1.1 lb
papad (thin, crisp, sun-dried wafers of dal flour), 8.8 oz,
    eaten as a snack or served sprinkled on soup
biscuits, 3.5 oz
corn-flour crackers, 3.5 oz
extruded noodles, 3.5 oz
rice-flour crackers, 1.8 oz
wheat-starch crackers, 1.8 oz

Prepared Food: $1.94
khaman (sweet, steam-baked chickpea cakes), 1.1 lb
Maggi 2-minute noodles, 7 oz
Everest chhole masala (chickpea masala), 3.3 oz
poori (fried wheat-flour flat breads), 3 pieces

Street Food: $3.07
chhole bhature (spicy chickpea curry with flat bread)
idli (steamed rice cakes)
pav bhaji (bread rolls with spicy mashed vegetables)
pizza, 1 small
uttapam (thick and crispy flat bread made with coconut
    milk), served with spicy vegetables
dosa (crispy savory pancake), 5, served with chutney or
    other spicy relishes
bhel poori (savory puffed rice with chutney)
tomato, cucumber, and onion sandwich, 1 small

Restaurants: $2.88
Shree Ganga Restaurant: dinner for four, including malai
    kofta (mashed potato dumplings in vegetable gravy)
navratan korma (fruits and vegetables cooked in a creamy
    sauce and flavored with herbs, spices, and cashews)
jeera fried rice (fried with cumin seeds)
tandoori roti (flat bread) cooked in a tandoor, or clay oven
fried dahl (lentil-flour flat bread)
papad
green salad
pickles
dessert

Beverages: $1.80
Thumbs Up cola, 2.1 qt
Godrej chai house tea, 5.3 oz
Nescafé Sunrise instant coffee, 0.5 oz
well water, for drinking and cooking

‡Not in photo

The Shipra River flows through the holy city of Ujjain, in the central Indian state of Madhya Pradesh. Every 12 years, millions of devout Hindus, including the Patkars, celebrate the month-long festival of Kumbh Mela by bathing in the Shipra's holy waters.

I n honor of the Hindu festival of Kumbh Mela, half the Patkars are on a month-long break from work and school in their city of Ujjain, in the central Indian state of Madhya Pradesh. But for Jayant Patkar, this is no break. He's a public works engineer with the city's water department, and the strain on Ujjain's water supply during this time is unparalleled. Many of the millions of Hindu pilgrims who come to the city during the festival stay for the entire month. Jayant's wife, Sangeeta, the principal of Oxford Junior College, is having a more relaxing time, as is their fifteen-year-old son Akshay. Their daughter Neha, nineteen, has time off from her studies but is cramming for the entrance exam to medical school. She'll race off on her scooter for a tutoring session right after her mother finishes cooking breakfast.

Sangeeta heats a thin film of vegetable oil in a frying pan, then adds mustard seed. When it sizzles, she tosses in thinly sliced potatoes, onions, and chopped chile peppers and stir-fries them until the onions are golden yellow. Previously, she has drained a pot of soaking *poha*—rice flakes—and set it aside to rest. Now, she adds the *poha* to the frying pan, along with a little sugar and salt, and a pinch of turmeric for color. After stir-frying the mixture a bit more, she covers it and puts the *poha* on the table with condiments—chopped cilantro with shredded dried coconut, and the crisp chickpea-flour noodles called *sev*. The Patkar family's breakfast is ready.

Everyone sits down to breakfast under a poster-size print of the Patkars' spiritual leader, Shri Parthasarathi Rajagopalachari. Sangeeta serves the *poha*, topping each mound of fluffy vegetables and rice with the coconut and cilantro, and sprinkles on the *sev*.

Meat is never served at their table. Like most Hindus, the Patkars are vegetarians. Fifteen-year-old Akshay doesn't like many vegetables, especially the gourds and squashes common in India, but because his family eats this way, he does as well. He has eaten chicken, he admits, and likes it.

Dietary restrictions notwithstanding, what all of India loves is a snack—the nation has thousands of street vendors. *Chhole bhature*

FACTS ABOUT INDIA

Population of Ujjain: 430,669

Total annual health care expenditure per person in US$: $31

Physicians per 100,000 population: 60

Number of vegetarian Pizza Huts in the world and in India: 1/1

Population living on less than $2 a day: 80%

Undernourished population: 20%

Population with access to safe sanitation: 33%

(spicy chickpea curry with flat bread), steamed rice cakes, *pav bhaji* (spicy mashed vegetables in a bread roll), *uttapam* (thick and crispy flat bread made with coconut milk) with spicy vegetables, *dosa* (a crisp savory pancake) with chutney or other spicy relishes, *bhel poori* (savory puffed rice with chutney), curries of all types, *lassi* yogurt drinks, fruit juices, and, of course, *chai* (Indian spice tea). Although each region of this vast, ancient country has its own unique foods, to some extent the lines dividing the regions have become blurred due to India's increasingly mobile society.

Like most food markets in India, Ujjain's central market is a whirlwind of shoppers elbowing their way around hundreds of vendors. Cows, sacred to Hindus, wander with them.

PHOTOGRAPHER'S FIELD NOTE

India has over a billion people, and nearly three-quarters of them have no access to a toilet. Most people have to relieve themselves in the open or use communal toilets, which are usually little more than cesspools. With all those people defecating in the open, the amount of fecal matter in the air and water is staggering. So are the bacterial and viral counts. (Whenever I go to India, I always catch something from breathing the air.) India and Indians are impatient to join the developed world. The spread of cell phones, color TVs, and personal computers there is amazing. But the country will only truly enter the ranks of the well-off and healthy nations when, like the Patkars, every family has a toilet in the home.

Sangeeta Patkar's Poha
(Rice Flakes)

1 pound poha (rice flakes—roasted and polished rice that
   has been beaten into thin flakes)
1 tablespoon vegetable oil
1 teaspoon mustard seed
2 large onions, sliced thin
1 large potato, sliced
3 large green chilies, chopped
1 teaspoon sugar
1 pinch turmeric powder
Salt

GARNISH
5 to 6 sprigs cilantro, chopped
2 ounces shredded dried coconut
¹/₂ pound *sev* (crispy chickpea-flour noodles)

Soak the *poha* in a widemouthed container, then drain and let sit for 5 minutes.

As the *poha* soaks, heat the oil in a large frying pan. When hot, add the mustard seed. After it begins to sizzle, add the onion, potato, and chilies. Sauté this mixture, stirring occasionally, until it becomes golden yellow and the potatoes are cooked through.

Add the soaked *poha,* sugar, turmeric powder, and salt to taste. Stir fry for 2 minutes, then cover the pan and remove from the heat.

To serve, boil water in a large openmouthed container and put the covered pan of *poha* on top, like a double boiler, to keep it warm.

Serve and garnish each plate with cilantro, coconut, and *sev*.

The Patkars shop for vegetables and fruit at Ujjain's sprawling main market (above left, buying okra and tomatoes).

For treats, they frequent a downtown shop (left) that makes *khova* (partially caramelized condensed milk), a key ingredient in Indian sweets.

Sangeeta prepares a breakfast of *poha* (rice flakes, see recipe opposite) in her small, organized kitchen.

The Ukita family—Sayo Ukita, 51, and her husband, Kazuo Ukita, 53, with children Maya, 14 (holding chips) and Mio, 17—in their dining room in Kodaira City, Japan, with one week's worth of food. Cooking methods: gas stove, rice cooker. Food preservation: small refrigerator-freezer. Favorite foods—Kazuo: sashimi; Sayo: fruit; Mio: cake; Maya: potato chips.

ONE WEEK'S FOOD IN MAY: 37,699 YEN/$317.25 USD

Grains and Other Starchy Foods: $31.55
koshihikari rice, 5.5 lb
potatoes, 5.3 lb
Danish white bread, sliced, 1 loaf
white flour, 1.3 lb
sato imo (Japanese yam), peeled, 1.1 lb
udon noodles, 1.1 lb
sômen noodles, 14.1 oz
white sandwich bread, 12.4 oz
Nippn macaroni, 10.6 oz
soba noodles, 10.6 oz
FryStar7 bread crumbs, 8.1 oz

Dairy: $2.26
whole milk, 25.4 fl oz
Haruna yogurt, 12 oz
butter,‡ 8.8 oz

Meat, Fish, and Eggs: $99.80
rainbow trout, 2.6 lb
ham, 2.2 lb
eggs, 10
sardines, large, 1.3 lb
clams, 1.1 lb
octopus, 1.1 lb
Spanish mackerel, 1.1 lb
pork loin, 1 lb
tuna, sashimi, 15.5 oz
horse mackerel, 14.8 oz
saury (fish), 13.5 oz
Japanese smelt (fish), 13.1 oz
eel, 12.7 oz
albacore, sashimi, 11.9 oz
Hagoromo tuna, canned, 11.3 oz
pork, cubed, 11.3 oz
beef, 10.8 oz
pork, minced, 10.6 oz
pork, sliced, 10.6 oz
pork, thin sliced, 10.3 oz
bacon, 7.8 oz
beef korokke (beef and potato patties), frozen, 7.4 oz,
    used for children's lunch
sea bream, sashimi, 3.6 oz
Nozaki's new corned beef (mix of horse and beef meat),
    canned, 3.5 oz

Fruits, Vegetables, and Nuts: $81.43
watermelon, 9.9 lb
cantaloupe, 4.4 lb
yellow bananas, 2.8 lb
red apples, 2.4 lb
white grapefruit, 2.2 lb
strawberries, 1.7 lb
cherries, canned, 7 oz
yellow onions, 4.8 lb
green bell peppers, 4 lb
cucumbers, 3.5 lb
daikon, 3.3 lb
bitter gourd,‡ 2.8 lb
soft tofu, 2.2 lb
tomatoes, 2 lb
carrots, 1.2 lb
green peas, in pods, 1.1 lb
broccoli, 1 lb
lettuce, 1 head
spinach, fresh, 1 lb
edamame, frozen, 14.1 oz
asparagus, 10.6 oz
green beans, frozen, 10.6 oz
mixed vegetables, frozen, 10.6 oz
bamboo shoots, 8.8 oz
white asparagus, canned, 8.8 oz
scallions, 8 oz
daikon sprouts, 6 oz
shitake mushrooms, 6 oz
wakame (seaweed), fresh, 5.6 oz
bean curd, fried, 1.8 oz
nori (seaweed), dried, 1.8 oz
wakame,‡ dried, 1.8 oz

Condiments: $28.28
white sugar, 15.6 oz
Ebara BBQ sauce, 9.9 oz
white miso, 9.9 oz
margarine,‡ 8.8 oz
Honen salad oil, 8.5 fl oz
sesame oil, 7.1 oz
bean sauce, 6 fl oz
ginger, 6 oz
Tea Time Mate sugar, 28 0.2-oz packs
Kyupi mayonnaise, 5.6 oz
Hinode cooking sake, 4.7 fl oz
Hinode mirin (low-alcohol rice wine for cooking), 4.7 fl oz
soy sauce, 4.7 fl oz

Sudo orange marmalade, 4.7 fl oz
Sudo strawberry jam, 4.7 fl oz
vinegar, 4.7 fl oz
Fuji oyster sauce, 4.2 oz
Bull Dog tonkatsu sauce, 3.4 fl oz
Captain Cook coffee creamers, 20 0.2-fl-oz packs
salt, 3.5 oz
Chinese spicy sauce, 2.9 oz, used on tofu
Kagome ketchup, 2.7 fl oz
sesame seed,‡ whole, 2.6 oz
honey, 2.5 oz
Pokka Shokutaku lemon juice, 2.4 fl oz
Momoya kimchi paste, 2.2 fl oz
soy sauce salad dressing, 2 fl oz
Ajinomoto olive oil, 1.8 fl oz
S&B hot mustard, 1.5 oz
S&B wasabi, 1.5 oz
white sesame seed, ground, 1.4 oz
black pepper,‡ 0.7 oz

Snacks and Desserts: $15.33
small cakes, 4
coffee break cookies, 1 lb
cream buns, 10 oz
Koikeya potato chips, 8.8 oz
Pasco cream rings, 8.8 oz
chiffon chocolate cake, 5.3 oz

Prepared Food: $21.78
Nissin cup of noodles, instant, 1.5 lb
Sapporo Ichiban noodles, instant, 1.1 lb
Showa pancake mix, 12.4 oz
Mama pasta meat sauce, canned, 10.4 oz
Oh My pasta meat sauce, canned, 10.4 oz
seaweed salad, dehydrated, 8.8 oz, add water to
    reconstitute
S&B golden hayashi sauce mix (Japanese-style beef
    bouillon cubes), 8.8 oz
Chinese dumplings,‡ frozen, 8.5 oz, used for the
    children's lunches
Ajinomoto hondashi soup base, bonito (fish) flavor, 5.3 oz
soup, instant, 2.7 oz
yaki fu (baked rolls of wheat gluten, wheat powder, and
    rice powder), 2.7 oz, eaten in soup
vegetable and seaweed rice ball mix, 1.3 oz
Riken seaweed rice ball mix, 1.2 oz
Kyowa egg drop soup, instant, 0.9 oz

(continued)

Beverages: $28.40
Kirin beer, 6 12-fl-oz cans
Coca-Cola, 2.1 qt
Nacchan orange soda, 2.1 qt
Suntory C.C. lemon joyful vitamin C soda, 2.1 qt
Ban Shaku sake, 1.8 qt
Coffee Break instant coffee, 2.5 oz
green tea, 2.1 oz
Alpha wheat tea, 2 oz
Afternoon Tea darjeeling black tea, 1.8 oz
tap water for drinking and cooking

Miscellaneous: $8.42
Mild Seven super-light cigarettes, 4 packs, smoked
　　by Kazuo

‡Not in photo

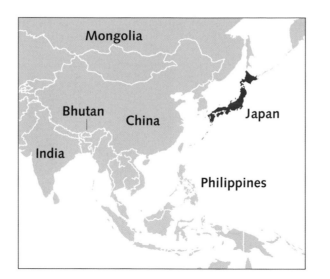

FACTS ABOUT JAPAN

Population of Metro Tokyo: 33,750,000

Population of Kodaira City: 175,585

Total annual health care expenditure per person in US$: $2,823

Population age 20 and older with diabetes: 6.7%

Fish consumption per person per year: 146 pounds

Exemplifying Japan's lively and adventurous food culture, Osaka's Dotomburi Street offers an all-squid eatery, an all-crab place, and a restaurant specializing in *fugu* (poisonous blowfish).

Sayo Ukita is up early, scrambling eggs and preparing small breakfast salads of artfully placed tomato, cucumber, and lettuce for her daughters Mio, seventeen, and Maya, fourteen. Ignoring the elegant spread, her husband Kazuo grabs a cup of coffee and a cigarette, turns on the television, and immerses himself in the baseball scores and the weather report before walking to the train station. Kazuo will have an hour-long commute into central Tokyo from the suburb of Kodaira City to the book warehouse where he works. The Ukitas own a car, but it's impractical to drive into the city.

Both girls slouch over the low table in the living room, sipping cups of tea, as Sayo serves their breakfast and then kneels to eat her own. Neither daughter is expected to pick up her breakfast dishes. "Their responsibility is to do well in school," says Sayo as she cleans up after them.

Sayo has already prepared Maya's two school-lunch bento boxes with food she cooked along with last night's dinner. In one, pieces of grilled fish and lightly steamed green beans flank a portion of white rice, all arranged with perfect symmetry. The second box holds four whole strawberries, two red cherries, and thin slices of Fuji

The girls head to the train station for trips in opposite directions, and Sayo will soon follow to do the day's shopping. Japanese train stations serve as the nucleus of Tokyo's suburban cities and are surrounded by shops and restaurants. The streets are quiet. Sayo and the other housewives in her neighborhood silently ride their bikes toward the train station to buy the freshest food they can find. Sayo will spend over an hour preparing dinner. The belief that the presentation is as important as the food itself extends from the finest department store to the humblest home in Japan.

Walking in Tokyo's hip Harajuku area (left), a small child clutches a kurepu—a crepe.

As might be expected in an island nation, Japanese families eat a wide variety of seafood: fish, shellfish, and seaweed of all kinds. In any given week, the Ukitas (Sayo at the supermarket; below) will eat at least a dozen different kinds of fish and shellfish and three varieties of seaweed. Like most people in this heavily urban country, the Ukitas also eat out often.

apple spread out like a fan. Sayo covers the two bento boxes and slips them into Maya's backpack, along with her chopsticks.

Mio will eat lunch with her friends at one of the many fast-food restaurants near her school—McDonald's, Mos Burger, Lotteria, KFC, DomDom, Wendy's, or Yoshinoya. Unlike the western fast-food companies whose food offerings generally stay the same year-round, menus at Japanese chains, such as Mos Burger, change with the season. Eating seasonally is a longstanding Japanese tradition, both to get foods at their most flavorful and because foods that are out of season are even more expensive than the normally high prices in this island nation.

FISH

According to Carl Safina of the Blue Ocean Alliance, one-third of humankind lives within fifty miles of a coast, and hundreds of millions more have their homes near lakes and rivers. Fish and other fruits of the sea are a mainstay of the diets in many cultures, but *Homo sapiens*'s love for seafood is imperiling aquatic ecosystems worldwide. The abundance pictured in these images, ecologists warn, may not survive this century.

Parrotfish • Okinawa, Japan

Hamsi • Istanbul, Turkey

Arctic char • Eastern Greenland

Prawns in corn cakes • Colombo, Sri Lanka

Swordfish • Palermo, Italy

Mackerel • Campeche, Mexico

King threadfin • Agats, Papua

Tilapia from the Niger River • Kouakourou, Mali

Frozen Tuna at Tsukiji auction • Tokyo, Japan

Scallops and bar • Neuilly, France

Dried fish from Lake Victoria • Kampala, Uganda

Snapper • Ginowan City, Okinawa

LIFE EXPECTANCY (in years)

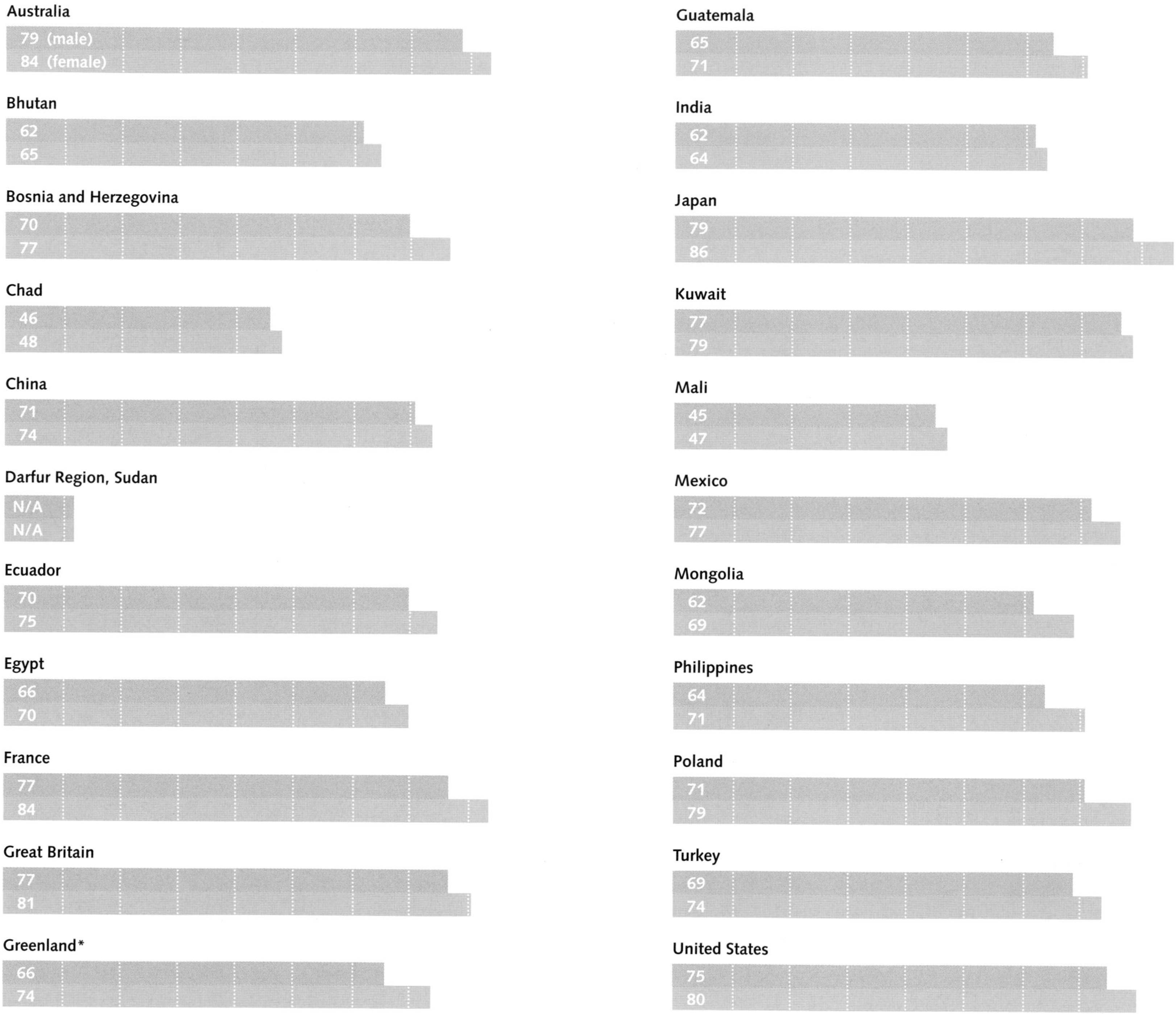

Australia
79 (male)
84 (female)

Bhutan
62
65

Bosnia and Herzegovina
70
77

Chad
46
48

China
71
74

Darfur Region, Sudan
N/A
N/A

Ecuador
70
75

Egypt
66
70

France
77
84

Great Britain
77
81

Greenland*
66
74

Guatemala
65
71

India
62
64

Japan
79
86

Kuwait
77
79

Mali
45
47

Mexico
72
77

Mongolia
62
69

Philippines
64
71

Poland
71
79

Turkey
69
74

United States
75
80

Source: World Health Organization's World Heath Statistics (2007)
N/A = Information not available
*Greenland source: CIA World Factbook (2007)

ACCESS TO SAFE WATER (% of total population)

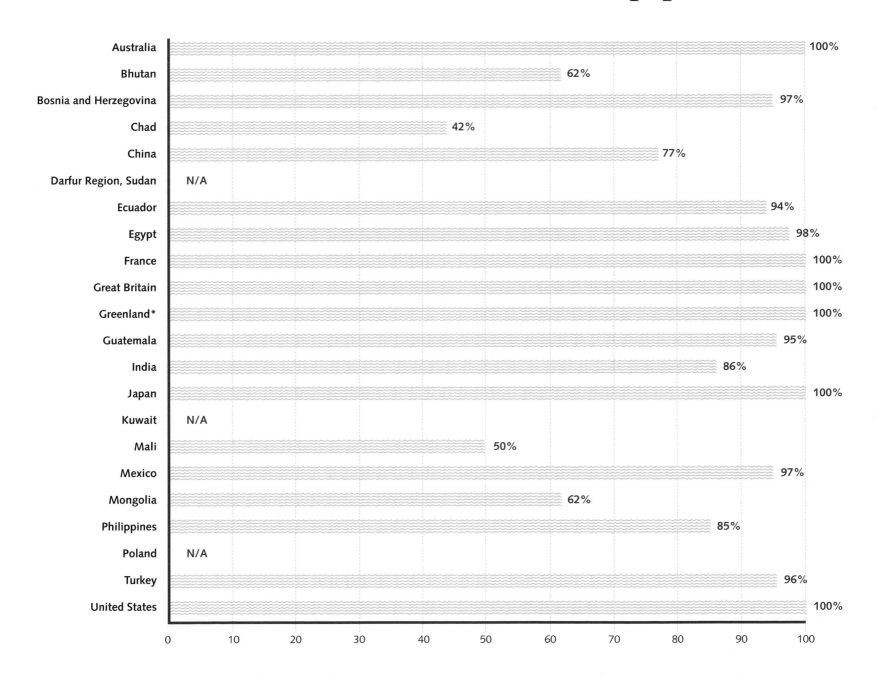

Australia	100%
Bhutan	62%
Bosnia and Herzegovina	97%
Chad	42%
China	77%
Darfur Region, Sudan	N/A
Ecuador	94%
Egypt	98%
France	100%
Great Britain	100%
Greenland*	100%
Guatemala	95%
India	86%
Japan	100%
Kuwait	N/A
Mali	50%
Mexico	97%
Mongolia	62%
Philippines	85%
Poland	N/A
Turkey	96%
United States	100%

Source: Human Development Report (2007–8)
N/A = Information not available
*Greenland source: Correspondence with Chief Medical Officer (2003)

Kuwait THE AL HAGGANS OF KUWAIT CITY

The Al Haggan family and their two Nepali servants in the kitchen of their home in Kuwait City, Kuwait, with one week's worth of food. Standing between Wafaa Abdul Aziz Al Qadini, 37 (beige scarf), and Saleh Hamad Al Haggan, 42, are their children, Rayyan, 2, Hamad, 10, Fatema, 13, and Dana, 4. In the corner are the servants, Andera Bhattrai, 23 (left), and Daki Serba, 27. Cooking methods: gas stoves (2), microwave. Food preservation: refrigerator-freezer.

ONE WEEK'S FOOD IN APRIL: 63.63 DINAR/$221.45 USD

Grains and Other Starchy Foods: $21.20
Kitco basmati rice, 11 lb
potatoes, 6.6 lb
hot dog rolls, 3.7 lb
Iranian bread, 3.4 lb
Normal white toast bread, sliced, 2 loaves
Patent all-purpose white flour, 2.2 lb
Kellogg's corn flakes, 1.1 lb
macaroni, 1.1 lb

Dairy: $19.37
Almarai laban (fresh drinkable yogurt), low fat, 2.1 qt
yogurt, 2.3 lb
chocolate milk, 25.4 fl oz
cream, 1.7 lb
Kraft Cheddar cheese, 1.7 lb
Kraft soft cream cheese spread, 1.1 lb
Carnation milk, powdered, 14.1 oz

Meat, Fish, and Eggs: $49.73
chickens, 5 whole, 11 lb
leg of lamb, 6.6 lb
zobaidy (fish), 5.4 lb
eggs, 30
Kabir Al Hajim Americana jumbo hamburger patties, 2.2 lb
Sadia chicken nuggets, 13.2 oz
chicken steak, frozen, 13.1 oz

Fruits, Vegetables, and Nuts: $46.59
oranges, 13.2 lb, half for juicing, half for eating
lemons, 4.4 lb
apples, 2.3 lb
dates, 2.2 lb
yellow bananas, 2.2 lb
strawberries, 1.7 lb, from Egypt
carrots, 12 lb
cucumbers, 6.6 lb
red onions, 6.6 lb
cabbage, 2 heads, from Jordan
zucchini, 3.3 lb
lettuce, 3 heads, from Egypt
cauliflower, 1 head
tomatoes, 2.2 lb
green bell peppers, 1.8 lb
California Garden Golden Sweet whole-kernel corn,
    canned, 1 lb
California Garden mushrooms, canned, 1 lb
salad greens, 2 bunches

Condiments: $39.68
white sugar, 4.4 lb
Dalal pure corn oil, 2.1 qt
Vimto fruit cordial syrup, 24 fl oz, used for nonalcoholic
    fruit drinks
Kroger Hot 'n' Zesty BBQ sauce, 1.1 lb
Consul olive oil, 16.9 fl oz
cilantro, 3 bunches
Heinz tomato ketchup, 12 oz
Galaxy Smooth and Creamy chocolate spread, 10.9 oz
Fountain pepper steak sauce, 10.6 fl oz
Kalas salt, 8.8 oz
black pepper, 7.1 oz
cassia powder, 7.1 oz
cloves, 7.1 oz
mixed Kuwaiti spices, 7.1 oz
Taebah cinnamon, 7.1 oz
Taebah garlic powder, 7.1 oz
mint, fresh, 2 bunches
mesquite sauce, 6 fl oz
ginger seed, 5.3 oz
Taebah cardamom, 5.3 oz
Rajah curry powder, 3.5 oz
Rajah ginger, ground, 3.5 oz
turmeric powder, 3.5 oz
dill, fresh, 1 bunch
Crystal hot sauce, 3 fl oz

Snacks and Desserts: $12.51
McCain Golden Long French fries, frozen, 3.3 lb
Hit biscuits, 1.1 lb
Ritz crackers, 14.1 oz
Pringles Original potato chips, 6 oz
Mars candy bars, 2.1 oz
Snickers candy bars, 2.1 oz
Twix candy bars, 2.1 oz
Bounty candy bars, 2 oz
Maltesers chocolate candies, 1.3 oz
Kit Kat candy bars, 0.7 oz

Prepared Food: $5.97
Maggi chicken noodle soup, 14.1 oz
Sadia breaded vegetable nuggets, frozen, 13.2 oz
Maggi dry soup, 7.2 oz.

Beverages: $26.40
bottled water, 7.9 gal
apple and apricot juice, 8 4.2-fl-oz boxes
Areen apple juice, 1.1 qt
Junior Drink mango and vitamins juice, 8 4.2-fl-oz boxes
mango juice, 6 5.6-fl-oz boxes
Sunquick orange juice concentrate, 28.4 fl oz
Nescafé, 1.8 oz
Lipton yellow label tea, 50 teabags

Because of its vast oil wealth, Kuwait helps pay for nearly every part of its people's lives—employment, health, education, housing, even food at some grocery stores. The government also provides a job to virtually every Kuwaiti citizen, women included. Saleh Hamad Al Haggan works for the nationally owned Kuwait Oil Company, while his wife, Wafaa Abdul Aziz Al Qadini, is a school inspector for the education ministry.

The oldest Al Haggan children, Hamad and Fatema, eat their usual breakfast of salty olives, tomatoes, cucumber, eggs, feta, Laughing Cow and Kraft cheeses, and fresh, chewy Iranian flatbread, then take the house elevator to their bedrooms in the upper reaches of their newly built home in Kuwait City. As they leave, the Nepali servant Daki Serba watches, amused, as Wafaa tries to tempt her youngest daughter, two-year-old Rayyan, with forkfuls of tomato omelet. Dana, four, who is also still at the table, eats with so much enthusiasm that Wafaa is thinking of putting her on a diet. As both little girls drink their milk tea, Daki and Wafaa discuss today's lunch: lamb *biryani*. They speak in Arabic, which Daki has learned since she's come to Kuwait.

Wafaa makes out a shopping list: Egyptian strawberries, Heinz ketchup, Kraft mayonnaise, Carnation powdered milk, Galaxy chocolate spread, Consul olive oil, and Jordanian cabbages. Most of the food in this oil-rich but soil- and water-poor country is imported, as are the laborers who come as service and industry personnel and as domestic helpers. Guest workers, who outnumber Kuwaiti residents, cannot become citizens. The Al Haggans hired Daki and the family's other Nepali servant, Andera Bhattrai, through an agency, along with Rayyan's nanny.

Wafaa leaves the two girls with Daki and takes the elevator upstairs to put on a new headscarf (Muslim women in Kuwait must dress modestly, yet they have more personal choice than the women in many other Arab countries). Her husband and the servants are the only ones who use the staircase. She grabs the keys to her late-model American-made minivan for the drive across town to her favorite supermarket. Although Kuwait imports 98 percent of its food, much of it from thousands of miles away, the choice and quality of the goods on display easily match those in European or U.S. markets, and the prices are lower. Despite the convenience and selection at the government-run shopping center, though, Wafaa goes to a small

"We never forget" say the signs posted all over Kuwait City, referring to the Iraqi invasion in 1991 and the country's liberation by a U.S.-led coalition.

Although Kuwait imports 98 percent of its food, much of it from thousands of miles away, the choice and quality of the goods on display easily match those in European or U.S. markets, and the prices are lower.

Most Kuwaitis do their grocery shopping in one of the country's many Western-style supermarkets.

shop for one of the most crucial components of her family larder—bread. A plate of *nan-e barbari*, Persian-style flat bread, accompanies every meal in Kuwait.

Today being Friday, the Muslim weekend, ten-year-old Hamad walks to the neighborhood mosque for noon prayer. "The supermarket near the mosque is an added incentive for attendance," says Wafaa, laughing. "I tell him, if he goes to the mosque, he can go to the super-market afterward and buy anything he wants." What does he want? More often than not, something from the global marketplace—Snickers, Twix, Mars, and Pepsi.

Despite the convenience and selection at the supermarket, Wafaa goes to a small shop for one of the most crucial components of her family pantry—flat bread.

Wafaa Al Haggan's Chicken Biryani

4 cups basmati rice
$1/2$ cup corn oil
2 cups shredded onion
1 tablespoon crushed garlic
$1/2$ teaspoon grated fresh ginger
1 whole chicken, cut into 10 pieces
Salt
1 tablespoon ground coriander seed
1 teaspoon turmeric
3 teaspoons allspice
1 cup yogurt
1 cup chopped fresh tomato
1 tablespoon freshly squeezed lemon juice
2 tablespoons ghee (clarified butter)
1 teaspoon saffron, soaked 10 minutes in warm water

GARNISH
1 cup shredded onion, fried until crispy
$1/4$ cup pine nuts, toasted
$1/4$ cup raisins, fried
$1/8$ cup cashews, fried

Rinse the rice, soak in water for 30 minutes, and drain. Preheat the oven to 350°F.

Heat a wide, shallow pan until hot; add the oil. When the oil is hot, add the onion, garlic, and ginger and sauté until the onion is translucent.

Add the chicken, salt to taste, coriander seed, turmeric, 1 teaspoon of the allspice, and the yogurt, tomato, and lemon juice. Stir over moderate heat for 7 minutes, taking care to prevent the mixture from boiling. Add water to cover; cook at a high simmer for 45 minutes.

Boil the rice in water with 1 tablespoon of salt for 5 minutes, then drain.

Put 1 cup of the rice in a pot, add the chicken mixture, then cover with half of the remaining rice. Top with the *ghee*, saffron, remaining allspice, and remaining rice.

Cover the pot with aluminum foil and the pot lid. Cook for 45 minutes. Remove from the oven, stir to combine, and sprinkle on the garnish.

Because 98 percent of the food in Kuwait is imported, Wafaa's kitchen is a snapshot of the world's market basket (opposite, top). Yet the diverse breakfast mix of Western (tomato omelet) and Eastern (cucumber salad, olives) is not enough to tempt fussy 2-year-old Rayyan (above). Most of the family's dinners still center around traditional Arab foods like lamb *biryani* (opposite, bottom; see recipe for chicken *biryani*).

Mali THE NATOMOS OF KOUAKOUROU

The Natomo family on the roof of their mud-brick home in Kouakourou, Mali, with a week's worth of food. Cooking method: wood fire. Food preservation: natural drying. Favorite foods—the Natomo family doesn't think in terms of "favorites."

ONE WEEK'S FOOD IN JANUARY: 17,670 FRANCS/$26.39 USD

Grains and Other Starchy Foods: $11.77
corn, dried, 66.2 lb
millet, 44.1 lb
rice, smoked, 44.1 lb

Dairy: $0.30
sour milk, 1.1 gal

Meat, Fish, and Eggs: $1.49
fish, dried, 4.4 lb, used in fish and okra soup when the family can afford it, otherwise, they have soup with okra only

Fruits, Vegetables, and Nuts: $6.50
tomatoes, 5.5 lb
okra, dried, 4.4 lb
onions, fresh, 2.2 lb
onions, dried, 1.1 lb
red chile peppers, dried, 14.1 oz
Anna d'Italie tomato paste, canned, 14 oz • This is not a common purchase, although they like to buy it when they can afford it.
No fruits were in season at the time the photograph was taken. In season, they have mangos from the ten trees planted by Sumana's father. Oranges from the market are also purchased if they can afford them.

Condiments: $6.03
vegetable oil, 1.1 gal
salt, 5.5 lb
tamarind, 2.2 lb
white sugar, 7.3 oz
sumbala (spice from nere tree pods), 3 lb, used as a bouillon for soup, mixed with chile pepper and dried onion and cooked with smoked rice

Prepared Food: $0.30
Maggi bouillon cubes, 2.1 oz • The family purchased this, but they normally use the traditional sumbala.

Homemade Food:
ngome, approx. 4 lb, thick fried cake made of millet flour, water, vegetable oil (and an inadvertent bit of sand)

Beverages:
water, drawn from community well for drinking and cooking

Family members: Soumana Natomo, 46 (in blue), sits flanked by his two wives, Fatoumata Toure, 33 (on his left), and Pama Kondo, 35 (on his right). Soumana and Fatoumata's children are daughter Tena, 4 months (in Fatoumata's lap); daughter Fourou, 12 (in front of her mother); son Kansy, 4 (in Soumana's lap); and son and daughter Mama, 8, and Fatoumata, 10 (both at their father's feet). Soumana and Pama's children are son Mamadou, 10 (in front of his mother); son Mama, 13 (far left); and son and daughter Kantie, 16, and Pai, 18 (far right). To Pama's right is Kadia Foune, 33, Soumana's sister-in-law, with her children Kantie, 1 (in her lap), and Mariyam, 8. They are living with the Natomos while Kadia's husband works in Ivory Coast.

A young boy balances a tray of fresh watermelon slices on his head as he walks through Kouakourou seeking buyers.

The village of Kouakourou—north of Mali's capital, Bamako, on the Niger River—looks as though it might have risen one day from the depths of the desert. The houses and court-yard walls blend in with the earth around them: desert-colored, sun-dried mud bricks, stuck together with mud mortar and plastered with . . . mud. There is no electricity. Inside the houses, the windowless rooms are cool and bare, containing only a sleeping mat or two, and sometimes a cushion or a stool. A high-walled courtyard—for cooking, mealtimes, and general daily life—surrounds each house, and beyond that is a common area where the women and girls pound grain in a mortar, singing to pass the time.

In two of the houses live co-wives Pama and Fatoumata Natomo. Between them, Pama and Fatoumata have one husband and nine children to feed. The women get along: "What Soumana does for one of us," says Pama, "he does for the other. If you see women fighting, it's usually because their husband is not treating them equally." For Pama, the bottom line is economic: "When you are married to the same man, if the wives don't get along, it makes too many problems in the family. It can really reduce the earnings."

Breakfast at the Natomos begins well before sunrise with the lighting of the morning fire in Pama's courtyard. Although the two co-wives each have their own home, they spend most of their waking hours here. Today, it's Fatoumata's turn to cook. Roosters provide the accompaniment to the rhythmic swooshing of the millet against the basket as she rocks it back and forth to winnow out the chaff. She pours water over the grain from a large cask, discards the debris that floats to the surface, pours off the water, and dumps the millet into the cooking pot, then adds fresh water and stirs. The porridge—called *tô*—is not as thick as other African grain foods, like *aiysh* (page 36), and is eaten with a soup or saucelike accompaniment (today it's salt, oil, and tamarind). Both families eat all their meals at Pama's house, which Fatoumata says is another key to the two women's good relationship. "We make a point of being together," says Fatoumata.

Pama's son Kantie, age sixteen, goes to boarding school about

In the predawn light, with little Tena bundled onto her back, Fatoumata crouches in the street outside her apartment and lights a fire under the griddle she uses to cook thick pancakes made from finely pounded corn or millet flour, oil, and salt.

On market days, Fatoumata (bending over) works with her co-wife (Pama, center). They acquire and unload grain in bulk and then sell it in smaller quantities to individuals and families. Soumana spends much of his time overseeing his working wives. Occasionally, he makes a trip to their single-room storehouse to replenish the grain his wives are selling.

five hours upstream in the town of Mopti. When he's home, he's just as involved as the other boys in the household activities, which is to say, not much. Sons, like their fathers, spend much of their time visiting with each other in the shade of the closest tree or building. But the daughters in rural Mali have many responsibilities. Pai, age eighteen, and her sisters must pound grain, wash dishes and clothing in the Niger, gather firewood, and help their mothers cook.

Pai is getting married today and will move from Mali to her new husband's home in Ivory Coast. "Since Pai was young, she has done all that she has been asked to do," says Fatoumata. Tears wet her cheeks and run down over the decorative tattoo that follows her jaw line. "She took care of all our babies. Now someone's carrying her away. I'll miss her," she says. Fatoumata's son Kansy follows Pai around like a puppy. He'll miss her too.

Pai is marrying her first cousin, Baba Nientao, and by tradition she has been told about the match only this morning—the day of her marriage. Pai and Baba visit the government office to sign the official papers, and then their family elders visit the imam (Muslim prayer leader) to finish the agreement. Afterward, Soumana distributes small candies to the children waiting eagerly for this marriage custom. Tonight, Pai's girlfriends will hide her somewhere in the village, and the groom and his friends will find her. Tomorrow, dozens of girls will dance and sing, accompanied by a band of drummers, to honor the marriage.

As Fatoumata finishes preparing their food, Soumana returns from the other house and makes the first of the five Muslim daily prayers. The women pray as well, but out of sight, and not with Soumana. Soon afterward, the children all arrive for breakfast, rubbing sleepy eyes. The two families sit together on the ground near the cooking fire and dip their spoons into the communal porridge pot. All meals center on porridge: some days, a wife might prepare smoked rice porridge with sour milk and an okra soup with dried red

The morning that the family broke the news to Pai (seated, top left) that she was to marry her cousin, Baba (eating bread), they all had breakfast together in the courtyard of Soumana's house.

chile peppers and salt. Others, a cornmeal porridge and a smoked fish stew with tomatoes. The children help as they are asked, and no one seems concerned about whose mother is doing the asking.

PHOTOGRAPHER'S FIELD NOTE

We were never invited to sit and dine with the Natomo family, maybe because they eat most meals with their hands, out of a common pot, and they were afraid that we Westerners wouldn't like it. Or maybe there simply wasn't enough—there were never any leftovers. While we were visiting, one of Soumana's daughters, Pai, got married in a complicated traditional ceremony, followed by a party in the family compound. But no food at all was served to the guests. Kouakourou was an amazingly friendly and hospitable village, and the Natomos very friendly as well, but food was not part of their generous spirit.

After pounding rice into flour in a large wooden mortar, Pama Kondo (left) sifts it to get rid of any remaining hulls. Behind her, 10-year-old Fatoumata (daughter of Fatoumata, Pama's co-wife) does much the same with some sorghum. Can she foresee a day when she will no longer have to pound grain? "That's what children are for," she replies seriously.

Soumana wraps his head and face for protection against many different elements—the morning chill, blowing sand, and the hot sun.

By 11:00 A.M. on Saturday, Kouakourou's weekly market has transformed the usually quiet shoreline of this Niger River backwater into a throng of bustling, thatch-shaded stalls and sharp-prowed traders' boats from up and down the river. Soumana (upper left, in blue, arm outstretched in front of his rented storeroom) goes to the market every week to buy and sell grain with his two wives, Pama and Fatoumata.

Mexico THE CASALESES OF CUERNAVACA

The Casales family in the open-air living room of their home in Cuernavaca, Mexico, with a week's worth of food. Marco Antonio, 29, and Alma Casales Gutierrez, 30, stand with baby Arath, 1, between them. At the table are their older children, (left to right) Bryan, 5, and Emmanuel, 7. Cooking method: gas stove. Food preservation: refrigerator-freezer. Favorite foods—Marco Antonio: pizza; Alma: crab; Emmanuel: pasta; Bryan: crab and candy; Arath: chicken.

ONE WEEK'S FOOD IN MAY: 1,862.78 MEXICAN PESOS/$189.09 USD

Grains and Other Starchy Foods: $15.76
corn tortillas, 22.1 lb
bread rolls, 3.1 lb
Morelos white rice, 2.2 lb
potatoes, 2.2 lb
Bimbo white bread, sliced, 1 loaf
Kellogg's Special K cereal, 1.1 lb
Morelos pasta, 1.1 lb
La Moderna pasta, 14.1 oz
pan dulces (sweet bread), assorted, 8.8 oz
bread sticks,‡ 3.5 oz.

Dairy: $24.61
Alpura 2000 whole milk, 1.9 gal
Alpura sour cream, 2.1 qt
Yoplait yogurt, 1.1 qt
cheese, handmade, 1.1 lb
La Lechera condensed milk, canned, 14 oz
cottage cheese, 13.6 oz
Carnation evaporated milk, 12 oz
Manchego cheese, 8.8 oz
cream cheese, 6.7 oz
butter, 3.5 oz

Meat, Fish, and Eggs: $42.81
chicken, pieces, 15.4 lb
crab, 2.7 lb
eggs, 18
tilapia (fish), 2.3 lb
catfish, 2.2 lb
sausage, 6.6 oz, one month's worth shown in photo
FUD ham, 5.6 oz.

Fruits, Vegetables, and Nuts: $44.21
mangos, 13.2 lb
pineapples, 6.6 lb
watermelon, 6.6 lb
oranges, 5.5 lb
cantaloupe, 4.4 lb
guavas, 2.2 lb
quinces, 2.2 lb
yellow bananas, 2.2 lb
roma tomatoes, 6.6 lb
tomatillos, 6.6 lb
corn,‡ 4 ears
avocados, 7
chayote squash, 2.2 lb
Morelos beans, 2.2 lb

white onions, 2.2 lb
zucchini, 2.2 lb
La Costeña pickled jalapeño peppers, canned, 1.6 lb
green beans, 1.1 lb
jalapeño peppers, fresh, 1.1 lb
broccoli, 12.8 oz
garlic, 8.8 oz
chipotle peppers (smoked jalapeños), 7.1 oz.

Condiments: $9.37
Capullo canola oil, 2.1 qt
margarine, 15.9 oz
McCormack mayonnaise, 13.8 oz
salt, 8.8 oz
garlic salt, 3.2 oz
McCormack black pepper, 3.2 oz
cumin, 0.7 oz
bay leaves, dried, 0.5 oz.

Snacks and Desserts: $8.47
Rockaleta chile lollipops, 1.2 lb
Ricolino pasitas chocolate candy, 1.1 lb
Muecas ice cream pops, 1.1 qt
Gamesa crackers, 15.9 oz
Drums marshmallows, 12 oz
Rockaleta chili candy, 5.7 oz.

Prepared Food: $4.79
Doña Maria mole (savory sauce made from chocolate and chile), 2.1 lb
Knorr chicken bouillon, 3.2 oz.

Beverages: $39.07
Coca-Cola, 12 2.1-qt bottles
water, bottled, 5 gal
Victoria beer, 20 11.8-fl-oz bottles
Jumex juice, 1.3 qt
Gatorade Fierce Black Hurricane drink, 1.1 qt
Gatorade lime drink, 1.1 qt
Nescafé, instant, decaf, 7.1 oz
tap water, for cooking.

‡Not in photo

Note: Groceries for one week, before the Casales family closed their shop and Marco Antonio moved to the United States to find work.

Marco Antonio and his wife Alma, a former surgical nurse, used to live in a two-story, cement-block apartment outside Cuernavaca, fifty miles south of Mexico City. They ran a *changarro*—a mini convenience store—on the ground floor. On any given day, the family schedule revolved around their little store. Seven-year-old Emmanuel would tend to his brother Arath while Marco Antonio tended to his customers—mostly neighbors and friends—through the shop window over a glass-fronted case. It wasn't uncommon for Marco Antonio to scoop up Arath and hold him while working in the shop. If he left to run errands, Alma would take over, because the key to earning enough money was keeping the shop open throughout the day and evening.

Shopping for the week's worth of food at a big supermarket, Alma marches to the cash register, chomping on an apple and laughing at the absurdity of buying so much bread at once. Her order of tortillas at the *tortillería* across the street from her convenience store is just as irrational—she never buys tortillas, which don't keep well, in bulk.

At midday, Alma would cook the family lunch upstairs: usually rice and beans, and then chicken soup with cilantro, or a savory crab soup, or sometimes *tacos de carnitas* (pork tacos). Like most of her neighbors, Alma bought fresh corn tortillas every day from the *tortillería* nearby. When lunch was ready, she would bring it down to Marco Antonio in the shop, and the children would sit on the floor with their bowls in their laps to eat. In the early evening, they would enjoy *merienda*, a light meal served with bread and fruit.

As the children grew, so did their access to chips, candy, and other processed treats. Almost without exception, the Casaleses' meals were served with Coca-Cola. In a week's time, they drank more than twenty quarts of it. When Alma was a child, beans, pasta, rice, and tortillas were the mainstays of her family's diet, and there was no money for sugary or salty treats. But even as cash-strapped adults, Alma and Marco Antonio have had access to a wider variety of foods, including packaged, high-fat, high-calorie snacks.

Like the United States, Mexico is overeating and underexercising. Alma and Marco Antonio's family are no exception: "My mother and my mother- and father-in-law are overweight," Alma said. "And they all have diabetes." Alma, Marco Antonio, and their eldest son are also overweight. She worries that they, too, will become diabetic.

Over time, more and more small stores opened up in Alma and Marco Antonio's neighborhood. Big supermarkets were also moving into the community and drawing customers away. The couple wasn't getting enough business to justify staying open, but Marco Antonio had no other job options. Then Alma's father, an illegal immigrant who picks fruit in the United States, suggested Marco Antonio join him. The couple decided this might be the only way to win financial security. They made arrangement with a *coyote*—a smuggler—to sneak Marco Antonio across the border in exchange for a $3,000 fee. They didn't have to pay it all at once—they gave the *coyote* a down payment and promised to pay the rest later. Both fearful and hopeful, Marco Antonio left his family behind.

So far, the risk has not paid off. Marco Antonio works only twenty or thirty hours a week, at $5 an hour. He sends his meager paychecks to Mexico, where Alma makes the monthly payment to the *coyote* and uses the little that remains to buy food and pay expenses. "We don't eat the way we used to," says Alma, but they aren't eating any healthier either. They eat fewer fresh fruits and vegetables, but the snack foods and soft drinks to which they've grown accustomed have become a permanent part of their diet—though they're down to four quarts of Coke a week. Alma has moved the children into her mother's house. Her sister, who owns a tiny lunch counter nearby, takes care of the boys while Alma works part-time at a nearby market. Is Alma concerned about Marco Antonio? "Yes, I worry," she says, "but he worries too—that he's not making enough money for us." Might he try to find a different job? He's afraid, she says. "As he gets more familiar with the system [in the United States] I think he will move on, but it's difficult because he doesn't know the language." They talk on the phone once a month, and hang on to their hopes and dreams.

Alma cooks crab soup at her sister's restaurant for the patrons and her family.

In what may be a disappearing custom, shoppers throng Cuernavaca's daily public market, inspecting the alarmingly fresh meat.

FAMILY RECIPE

Alma Casales' Sopa de Jaiba
(Crab Soup)

2 ounces margarine
2 pounds red tomatoes, chopped
$1/2$ pound white onions, sliced
5 cloves garlic
5 olive leaves
5 tablespoons salt
$41/2$ pounds crab pieces, thoroughly rinsed
$11/2$ pounds La Costeña chipotle peppers
1 pound carrots, sliced
10 quarts water

In a large pan, melt the margarine. Add the tomatoes, onions, garlic, olive leaves, and salt. Fry until the onions soften. Add the crab, peppers, and carrots to the pot. Pour in the water, cover, and simmer for 1 hour and 20 minutes. Enjoy with Mexican white bread.

Mongolia THE BATSUURIS OF ULAANBAATAR

The Batsuuri family in their single-room home—a sublet in a bigger apartment—in Ulaanbaatar, Mongolia, with a week's worth of food. Standing behind Regzen Batsuuri, 44 (left), and Oyuntsetseg (Oyuna) Lhakamsuren, 38, are their children, Khorloo, 17, and Batbileg, 13. Cooking methods: electric stove, coal stove. Food preservation: refrigerator-freezer (shared, like the stoves, with two other families).

ONE WEEK'S FOOD IN MAY: 41,985.85 TOGROGS/$40.02 USD

Grains and Other Starchy Foods: $5.41
bread, 15.4 lb
potatoes, 11 lb
white rice, 4.4 lb
Macbur pasta, spirals, 2.2 lb
spaghetti, 2.2 lb
white flour, 2.2 lb.

Dairy: $6.19
Apta milk, 3.2 qt
Rama butter, 2.2 lb
Holland cheese,‡ 1.1 lb, not a common purchase, as it
    is expensive and considered a luxury item

Meat, Fish, and Eggs: $13.51
beef, 6.8 lb
mutton, 4.4 lb
eggs, 30
sausage, dried, 1.6 lb • Oyuna didn't find the kind she
    wanted so she bought less than usual.
kilka (an anchovy-like fish), canned, 7.1 oz
sprat (a herring-like fish), canned, 5.3 oz.

Fruits, Vegetables, and Nuts: $8.35
green apples, 4.4 lb
tangerines, 2.2 lb
cucumbers, 5.3 lb
cabbage, 1 head
carrots, 2.2 lb
tomatoes, 2.2 lb
turnips, 2.2 lb
yellow onions, 1.1 lb
Urbanek vegetables, preserved, 17.6 fl oz
garlic, 1.9 oz.

Condiments: $1.58
white sugar, 2.2 lb
vegetable oil, 16.9 fl oz
salt, 8.8 oz
ketchup, 4.4 oz
mayonnaise, 3.7 oz
Vitana soy sauce, 0.9 fl oz

Snacks and Desserts: $2.38
pastries, 6.6 lb
dried milk treat, 1.1 lb, extruded, sweetened, and dried
    milk, eaten as a sweet

Beverages: $1.74
Bavaria Millennium Brew beer, 3 14-fl-oz bottles • Regzen
    doesn't drink alcohol at home, but does with his friends.
Gita Indian black tea, 4.4 oz
tap water, for drinking and cooking

Miscellaneous: $0.86
Monte Carlo cigarettes, 2 packs

‡Not in photo

FACTS ABOUT MONGOLIA

Population of Ulaanbaatar: 812,000

Livestock population (cattle, horses, sheep, goats, camels): 30,500,000

Number of livestock deaths from drought and *zud* (brutal winter) between summer of 1999 and winter of 2002: 7,000,000

Land used for grazing (grassland and arid grazing): 80.7%

Population living in *gers*: 45%

Rank of Ulaanbaatar among the world's coldest capital cities: No. 1

Year in which Soviet economic aid stopped: 1991

Total annual health care expenditure per person in US$: $37

Population age 20 and older with diabetes: 3%

Population living on less than $2 a day: 75%

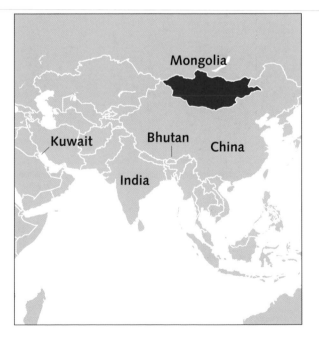

ountains of flour and imported sugar ring the big central market in Ulaanbaatar where Oyuntsetseg Lhakamsuren shops for her family's food. On spring mornings, she walks to the huge covered marketplace through a silvery mist of airborne flour that envelops the outdoor grain sellers. Inside, rows and rows of individual vendors sell their wares from tabletops and stalls. Oyuna, as she is called, shops briskly. She chooses yellow onions and garlic cloves at one kiosk and a jar of Chinese-style preserved vegetables at another. Red meat is a main part of the diet in Mongolia—as it is in most cold climates—and Oyuna is choosy, visiting four vendors before deciding on her mutton purchase. She counts out her *togrogs* (Mongolian currency) and stuffs the package into her oversized shopping bag. Before returning home, she takes a detour—to the local Buddhist temple. "We need help with many problems," she says, as she offers a coin with her prayer.

Until 1990, Mongolia's Soviet-style Communist government controlled the economy. Since then, many Mongols have found the country's new free-market system difficult to navigate; Oyuna's

The Soviet-style apartment blocks on the edge of Ulaanbaatar, a legacy of Mongolia's Communist past, are now surrounded by squatters—more accurately, urban homesteaders. Former nomads, they have precisely parceled out the land and staked out their neat *gers*. The *gers* lack indoor plumbing, but in other ways are more comfortable than the city's crowded apartments.

Oyuna shops briskly. She chooses yellow onions and garlic cloves at one kiosk and a jar of Chinese-style preserved vegetables at another. Red meat is a main part of the diet in Mongolia.

Dumpster-diving free-range cows show that Mongolians now have enough food to throw some away.

An apple-cheeked girl selling root vegetables waits for customers at Ulaanbaatar's central retail market.

family is among them. After stockpiling materials for years, her husband, Regzen Batsuuri, hand-built a house on squatter's land next to their traditional family *ger* (a round, portable tent structure) on the outskirts of the city. Meanwhile, Oyuna opened a small private pharmacy with former coworkers; they had worked together at a state pharmacy before the government began allowing private businesses. It was a heady time for the family, but more financially risky than they knew. Oyuna and her friends secured a private loan to support their pharmacy but didn't understand how interest would be added to the amount they borrowed. The debt built up, and Oyuna's family lost everything, including their *ger* and their house.

Inside the huge covered marketplace, rows and rows of individual vendors sell their wares from tabletops and stalls.

Regzen Batsuuri slices up squash, carrots, and cabbage (left) in the small kitchen his family shares with two other families. He has already prepared the *buuz* (mutton-stuffed dumplings; below) with the help of his daughter, Khorloo. Because Oyuntsetseg is working at her pharmacy tonight, Batbileg walks the meal over to her and then the three of them and a niece sit down to dinner (right).

The family of four now lives in a single room. It is in a modern apartment with running water, but it belongs to Tanya, an eighty-three-year-old Russian immigrant, who rents them the room and gives them kitchen privileges. Oyuna has opened a new, much smaller dispensary. Regzen, now an electrician, longs for their old homestead, but the children and Oyuna are happy to have an indoor bathroom and an electric stove, even if it means that they're all crowded into the same small room. Best of all, the children say, they don't have to haul buckets of water up a steep hill to their home any more.

Philippines THE CABAÑAS OF MANILA

The Cabaña family in the main room of their 200-square-foot apartment in Manila, Philippines, with a week's worth of food. Seated are Angelita Cabaña, 51, her husband, Eduardo Cabaña, 56 (holding sleeping grandson Dave, 2), and their son Charles, 20. Eduardo, Jr., 22 (called Nyok), his wife, Abigail, 22, and their daughter, Alexandra, 3, stand in the kitchen. Behind the flowers is the youngest son, Christian, 13 (called Ian). Cooking method: gas stove. Food preservation: none.

ONE WEEK'S FOOD IN JANUARY: 2,629.50 PESOS/$49.42 USD

Grains and Other Starchy Foods: $7.09
white rice, 30.9 lb
Park n' Go white bread, sliced, 3 loaves
pan de sal (salty bread), 2.2 lb
cheese bread, 1.3 lb
potatoes, 11.6 oz
V.C. original breading mix, 3.5 oz

Dairy: $2.01
Nestlé Bear Brand milk, powdered, 12.7 oz
Kraft Cheez Whiz, 8.8 oz

Meat, Fish, and Eggs: $19.72
pork, 7.7 lb
chicken, whole, 4.4 lb
milk fish, fresh, 4.4 lb
galunggong (fish), fresh, 2.2 lb
tilapia (fish), fresh, 2.2 lb
eggs, 12
foot-long hot dogs, 1.1 lb
Ma Ling's luncheon meat, canned, 14.1 oz
555 Brand sardines, in hot tomato sauce, canned, 5.8 oz
555 Brand sardines, in tomato sauce, canned, 5.8 oz
tuyo (assorted dried fish, such as tamban), 2.5 oz

Fruits, Vegetables, and Nuts: $7.17
green mandarin oranges, 8.8 lb
yellow bananas, 4.4 lb
saba plantains, 2.9 lb
limes, 8.8 oz
kalabasang tagalog (squash), 2.9 lb
eggplants, 2.4 lb
green tomatoes, 2.2 lb
daikon, 2.2 lb
squash, 1.7 lb
kangkong (water spinach), 1.3 lb
bitter gourd, 1.1 lb
red onions, 1.1 lb
cabbage, 1 small head
okra, 12.4 oz
carrots, 8.8 oz
mongo beans, 8.8 oz
snap beans, 8.8 oz
sweet potato, 6.5 oz
hot green peppers, 5.3 oz
garlic, 3.7 oz

Condiments: $2.01
white sugar, 2.2 lb
cooking oil, 1.1 lb
Silver Swan soy sauce, 11.8 fl oz
tamarind, 8.8 oz
Lorins Patis hot fish sauce, 5.9 fl oz
ketchup, 5.6 oz
vinegar, 5.1 fl oz
salt, 4.4 oz
Mang Tomas all around sauce (made from ground liver mixed with seasonings), 2.9 fl oz
black pepper, 0.5 oz
bay leaves, 8

Snacks and Desserts: $1.92
Granny Goose stone-ground tortilla chips, 8.5 oz
graham crackers, 3.5 oz
Sky Flakes crackers, 3.5 oz
Hello chocolate mini bars, 2.1 oz
chocolate candies, 1.1 oz
Halls cough drops, 1 oz

Prepared Food: $1.13
Lucky Me instant pancit canton noodles, 1.3 lb
Nissin instant ramen noodles, 1.3 lb

Fast Food: $1.86
Jollibee burger and French fries
fried chicken and rice
Coca-Cola, 2 cups

Street Food: $1.30
siopao (steamed pork buns), 1.1 lb
quek quek (hard-boiled quail eggs covered in flour and egg mixture and deep-fried), 5.3 oz

Beverages: $4.46
Pop Cola, 11 27-fl-oz bottles, produced by the *Coca-Cola* brand
Sunkist orange juice drinks, 4 8.5-fl-oz packs
Nescafé instant coffee, 1.9 oz
tap water for drinking and cooking from indoor faucet from 2 to 6 A.M. only; very weak water pressure

Miscellaneous: $0.75
HOPE cigarettes, 2 packs

FACTS ABOUT PHILIPPINES

Population of Metro Manila: 14,000,000 (est.)

Filipinos living or working overseas: 7,500,000 (est.)

Total annual health care expenditure per person in US$: $36

Population age 20 and older with diabetes: 7.1%

Number of Jollibee restaurants: 570

Population living on less than $2 a day: 48%

Jammed into the narrow valley between Manila Bay and the Sierra Madre Mountains, Metro Manila's more than fourteen million people, many of them very poor, use every square foot of available space.

To help keep her family fed, in school, and financially afloat, Angelita Cabaña does many jobs: demonstrating her line of Tupperware, providing massage therapy, and being the landlady for the half of the house she's given over to renters, squeezing her eight family members into three small rooms to do so. In a pinch she can also repair watches. Lita, as she is known, inherited a watch repair business when her father died, and that's the work her husband Eduardo does as well—in her father's tiny shop bolted to the sidewalk on a nearby street. On a good day, Eduardo earns about $18.

The Cabañas' neighborhood in the Malate District of Manila houses the working poor. Drug addicts, overflowing trash, lack of basic city services, and crime are visible reminders that creating a safe, healthy environment for a crowded, overwhelmingly poor population is an enormous challenge. But inside the Cabañas' small home, everything is orderly and clean, if threadbare.

Angelita's son Nyok, a graduate student in business administration, shares one small room with his wife, Abigail, and their two young children. Another grown son, Charles, also a student, lives with his parents as well. Many extended families in the city live together to share expenses. In addition, the Cabañas benefit from Lita's remarkable skill at the Manila game of making every peso count at the market—a game with many angles, the most important of which is having *sukis*.

Suki is the term used for both buyers and sellers and refers to people who do repeat business with one another. Over time, the relationship can provide deep discounts for the buyer and ensures the seller a steady customer. To Lita, the discount might mean the difference between buying a snack-size or a meal-size portion of some item. "I can get up to a 20 percent discount from my *sukis*," she says. Lita likes to survey the crowd of fruit and vegetable vendors before settling for the freshest produce that's within the budget. She buys onions and tomatoes from her *suki*, choosing only green tomatoes because "it takes longer for the green ones to spoil." Lita does the food shopping for the entire family between her massage appointments and Tupperware sales.

Fish vendors charge by the *tumpok* (pile).

A few blocks away from the Cabañas' home in the Malate shopping area, Angelita (at right), buys a week's worth of rice—30 pounds—for the photo shoot. Most small *sari-saris* (variety/convenience shops) have similar rails, or bars, for security.

Lita's budget doesn't always stretch enough to afford meat. "I try to serve nutritious food that is not too expensive, like vegetables and fish," she says, "but there are times when I can only serve them dried fish, or sardines. Every now and then we have extra money, and I get to buy roast chicken from a restaurant. We get by, and though our food may not be as expensive as what the rich people eat, it is just as delicious."

Though McDonald's, KFC, and other global food purveyors have made their way to Metro Manila, street food is a mainstay of the culture and an important part of its underground economy. *Isaw*—pig and chicken small-intestine barbecue—is a national favorite. *Dugo* is curdled and congealed pig blood, cut into chunks, skewered, and then grilled. *Adidas,* named after the running shoe, is barbecued chicken feet. Lita's youngest son, Ian, who lunches on the street each day, spends about 100 pesos ($1.80 USD) a week. Charles prefers to eat at McDonald's or Jollibee, a local fast-food chain that is going global. He says street food "will always remain a step ahead,

though, because of the affordability, accessibility, and of course the distinct flavor that is truly Pinoy (Filipino)."

Though the Cabaña family has spread out across the city during the day, everyone returns home to eat dinner together. Lita's children generally clamor for her *sinigang*, a sour, tamarind-flavored broth with fish, shellfish, pork, or beef. Charles claims it is the best in all the Philippines, and Ian calls it his favorite meal. "We have a very humble home," says Lita, "but we are proud to say that it is filled with love and respect. Education is our main priority—we tell our children this is all that they can inherit from us."

PHOTOGRAPHER'S FIELD NOTE

One evening we happened upon a tent pitched outside a house where a funeral was taking place. Standing next to her mother's glass-topped casket, the bereaved daughter was cooking up eggplant and dried fish on a small fire. She was serving the results to the friends and neighbors at the funeral, many of whom were taking advantage of a quirk in Filipino law that permits betting on games, but only at funerals. Part of the gaming proceeds went to help the daughter bury her mother.

Outside the Quiapo Market (below), people pick through the trash discarded from the early-morning wholesale market.

MEALS

As every traveler learns, human beings eat an extraordinary variety of foods prepared in stunningly diverse ways. Yet these pictures of meals around the world, apparently so dissimilar, illustrate a trend, says Francine R. Kaufman, pediatrician and author of the book *Diabesity: The Obesity-Diabetes Epidemic That Threatens America*. As societies around the world grow more affluent, their members eat more sugar, more refined carbohydrates, more dietary fat. Nutritionists disagree on the effects of each one, but most believe that the collective impact of this transition is disastrous—producing a global epidemic of obesity, diabetes, and cardiovascular disease.

Potato curry, dal, chapatis at Kumbh Mela • Ujjain, India

Cinnamon breakfast roll, cheese, meat • Bargteheide, Germany

Serrano ham, grilled vegetables, fruit • Paris, France

BBQ pork • Warsaw, Poland

Pork and onions • Brisbane, Australia

Chugchucaras (pork, bananas, corn, empanadas) • Latacunga, Ecuador

Karaoke lunch (chicken, crab, soup, spring rolls) • Manila, Philippines

Poha breakfast (rice flakes, chickpea-flour noodles) • Ujjain, India

Fried eggs • Sarajevo, Bosnia and Herzegovina

Chicken and rice • Dubai, United Arab Emirates

Plastic food, restaurant window • Kobe, Japan

Chicken, pigs' feet, beef, tofu, egg-white custard • Weitaiwu Village, China

Whataburger fried chicken and French fries • San Antonio, Texas, USA

LITERACY RATE (15 years and older)

COUNTRY	% of total population	
	male	female
Australia	99	99
Bhutan	60	34
Bosnia and Herzegovina	99	94
China	95	86
Chad	56	39
Darfur Region, Sudan	N/A	N/A
Ecuador	92	90
Egypt	83	59
France	99	99
Great Britain	99	99
Greenland	100	100
Guatemala	75	63
India	73	48
Japan	99	99
Kuwait	94	91
Mali	53	40
Mexico	92	90
Mongolia	98	97
Philippines	92	93
Poland	100	100
Turkey	95	80
United States	99	99

Source: CIA World Factbook (2000–2005)
N/A = Information not available

Young monks at the Gangte Goemba Monastery in Bhutan read holy Buddhist scripts in the cold morning air.

In Mongolia, Khorloo (center), Batbileg (reclining), and their cousin Suvd Erdene do their homework.

FERTILITY RATE

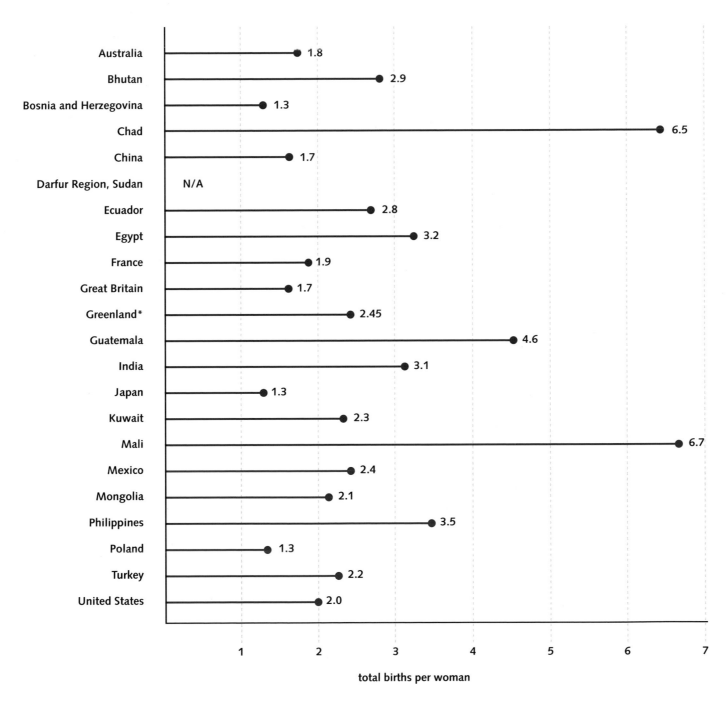

Australia	1.8
Bhutan	2.9
Bosnia and Herzegovina	1.3
Chad	6.5
China	1.7
Darfur Region, Sudan	N/A
Ecuador	2.8
Egypt	3.2
France	1.9
Great Britain	1.7
Greenland*	2.45
Guatemala	4.6
India	3.1
Japan	1.3
Kuwait	2.3
Mali	6.7
Mexico	2.4
Mongolia	2.1
Philippines	3.5
Poland	1.3
Turkey	2.2
United States	2.0

total births per woman

Source: UNDP Human Development Report (2007–2008)
N/A = Information not available
*Greenland source: Correspondence with Chief Medical Officer (2003)

Poland THE SOBCZYNSCY OF KONSTANCIN-JEZIORNA

The Sobczynscy family in the main room of their apartment in Konstancin-Jeziorna, Poland, outside Warsaw, with a week's worth of food. Marzena Sobczynska, 32, and Hubert Sobczynski, 31, stand in the rear, with Marzena's parents, Jan Boimski, 59, and Anna Boimska, 56, to their right and their daughter Klaudia, 13, on the couch. Cooking method: gas stove. Food preservation: refrigerator-freezer. (Polish surnames are gender-based and can change when speaking of the family as a whole. "Sobscynscy" is plural).

ONE WEEK'S FOOD IN JULY: 582.48 ZLOTYS/$151.27 USD

Grains and Other Starchy Foods: $11.02
mature potatoes, 6.6 lb, used for grilling
new potatoes, 4.4 lb
onion bread, 2.2 lb
Szymanowska flour, 2.2 lb
six-grain bread, 1.8 lb
bread rolls, 1.3 lb
sesame bread,‡ 1.3 lb
Polish bread, 1.3 lb
Agnesi spaghetti, 1.1 lb
baguettes, 1.1 lb
white rice, 1.1 lb
Sonko buckwheat, 14.1 oz
ciabatta bread, 10.6 oz
Wasa crispbread, 7.1 oz

Dairy: $19.50
Bakoma kefir (type of light sour cream), 1.6 qt
milk, 1.1 qt
feta cheese, 1.2 lb
cottage cheese, low fat, 15.9 oz
cottage cheese, small curd, whole milk, 15.9 oz
Danone Danio Straciatela cream cheese (contains vanilla
    cream and chocolate flakes), 15.9 oz
cream, 15.2 fl oz
Bakoma plum yogurt, 10.6 oz
Danone Fantasia cream cheese, 10.6 oz
gouda cheese, 8.8 oz
mozzarella cheese, 7 oz
Soignon cheese, 7 oz
Danone Danio vanilla cream cheese, low fat, 5.3 oz
Danone Danio strawberry cream cheese, 5.3 oz
Bakoma Kremowy coconut yogurt, 5.3 oz
Bakoma Kremowy coffee yogurt, 5.3 oz

Meat, Fish, and Eggs: $50.50
Auchan (store brand) pork knuckle, 4.3 lb
Auchan chicken, whole, 3.3 lb; fillet, 2.2 lb
Auchan pork loin with bone, 2.3 lb
Auchan pork, minced, 2.2 lb
Auchan pork shoulder, 2.2 lb
Auchan ribs, 2.2 lb
sausage, 2.2 lb
Auchan ham, 1.7 lb
eggs, 12
Lisner herring, 1.7 lb
head cheese, 1.5 lb
Koral Norwegian salmon, 1.1 lb

chicken pâté, 13.8 oz
 Losos sprat with tomato sauce, canned, 12 oz
smoked pork sausage, 11.6 oz
Auchan pork loin, 10.6 oz
mackerel, 10.6 oz
Morliny hot dogs, 8.8 oz

Fruits, Vegetables, and Nuts: $22.59
pears, 4.4 lb
lemons, 2.2 lb
red cherries, 2.2 lb
Dole yellow bananas, 2 lb
green apples, 1.1 lb
honey melon, 1.1 lb
plums, 1.1 lb
oranges, 1 lb
tomatoes, 11 lb
carrots, 3.3 lb
white onions, 2.2 lb
cucumbers, 2.1 lb
bell peppers, red, orange, yellow, 1.4 lb
butter lettuce, 2 heads
cauliflower, 1 head
pickles, 17.6 fl oz
mixed vegetables for soup stock (leek, parsley, carrots,
    celeriac), 1.1 lb
red onions,‡ 1.1 lb
radishes, 10.6 oz
tomato puree, 7.4 oz
chives, 3.5 oz
walnuts, 7.1 oz; hazelnuts, 5.3 oz

Condiments: $11.70
Sauerkraut, 4.4 lb
vegetable oil, 1.1 qt
white sugar, 2.2 lb
Winiary mayonnaise, 24 fl oz
margarine, 14.1 oz
olive oil, 12.7 fl oz
salt, 8.8 oz
basil, fresh, 1 bunch
mustard, 4.4 oz
Vegeta (mix of various herbs and salt), 4.4 oz
chile powder, 1.9 oz
cumin powder, 1.9 oz
rosemary, dried, 1.9 oz
sweet paprika, 1.4 oz
marjoram, 0.5 oz
bay leaf, dried, 0.2 oz.

Snacks and Desserts: $4.49
M&M's chocolate candy, 14 oz
Princessa Maxi chocolate bar, 6.4 oz
Milka chocolate candies with nuts, 5.3 oz
Mentos grapefruit candies, 4.3 oz
Alpen gold nussbeisser chocolate hazelnut bar, 3.5 oz
Mentos mints, 2.2 oz
Twix candy bar, 2.1 oz
Snickers candy bar, 2 oz
Danusia chocolate bar, 1.8 oz
Olza Prince Polo chocolate wafer, 1.8 oz

Prepared Foods: $0.88
Knorr chicken bouillon cubes, 8.7 oz

Fast Food: $2.60
McDonald's: hamburger, French fries, drink

Beverages: $21.28
mineral water, 1.2 gal
Dr. Witt carrot juice, 3 1.1-qt bottles
Zywiec Zdroj mineral water, 3.2 qt
Coca-Cola, 2.1 qt
Garden apple juice, 2 1.1-qt boxes
orange juice, 2 1.1-qt boxes
Miller beer, 4 12-fl-oz bottles
Sprite, 1.1 qt
coffee, 7.1 oz
Lipton tea, 50 teabags
tap water, for drinking and cooking

Miscellaneous: $6.71
Pedigree dog food, dry, 3 lb; canned, 2.8 lb
Wiskas cat food, canned, 2.8 lb; *Wiskas* cat food, dry, 1 lb

‡Not in photo

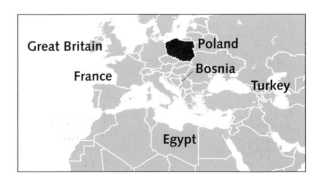

Beet soup with dumplings and herbs, potatoes, sauerkraut, meat stews simmered for days—Hubert Sobczynski grew up on this hearty Polish fare in a small village outside Warsaw. There is nothing in Polish cooking that even remotely resembles Japanese cuisine, but both the taste of sushi and the art of its preparation attracted him. After he apprenticed with a visiting Japanese sushi chef in Warsaw's first Japanese restaurant, he and his wife Marzena opened Shoku-Yoku, their own sushi eatery. To support the new restaurant and save for their own house, they moved with their thirteen-year-old daughter, Klaudia, into Marzena's parents' tiny three-room apartment.

FACTS ABOUT POLAND

Population of Konstancin-Jeziorna: 22,000

Total annual health care expenditure per person in US$: $411

Population age 20 and older with diabetes: 4.1%

In her farmhouse kitchen in the village of Adamka, in central Poland, 93-year-old Maria Kwiatkowska—Hubert's friend Borys's grandmother—slices the cheesecake she baked for the traditional family gathering on All Saints Day. After her children and grandchildren visit the graves of their relatives in the local cemetery, they will descend on her for a splendid lunch of noodle soup with cabbage and carrots, pork roast stuffed with prunes, pickled pumpkin, a fruit-nut roll, and cheesecake.

Scooping out sauerkraut, Marzena leads Hubert and Klaudia through the family's grocery shopping at the Auchan hypermarket. The huge new supermarket is a sign of the rapid economic development of Poland as well as private farming; two decades ago food production was dominated by communist-era collective farms, which were owned by the state.

In the mornings, the three pack their bedclothes into cupboards and tuck the beds back into the living room sofa. Then it's time for breakfast in the narrow kitchen. The morning meal consists of a variety of foods—sweet buns, fruit, yogurt, cereal and milk, eggs, sausage, and tea or coffee. Although the family, like most Poles, eats mostly traditional Polish fare at home, Marzena's mother Anna has developed a taste for Hubert's sushi.

Sushi is just one of many international cuisines to come to this formerly communist Eastern European country now that disposable income is increasing and people are beginning to eat outside their homes. Today, Poland is home to a cast of the usual multinational supermarkets, and food is also readily available from small groceries, green markets, butcher shops, and bakeries. Along with post-communist capitalism (privately run economic system), American-style fast food has come to Poland, and with it something that Marzena herself never experienced growing up—the media-fueled fear that teenage girls have of getting fat. It seems odd to Marzena that just as high-calorie fast food has been introduced into the culture, so has the desire to avoid its effects at all costs. "All of Klaudia's friends are on a diet," Marzena says. She worries that the struggle is not winnable.

Klaudia's attitudes and experiences concerning food differ sharply from her mother's. Marzena was a child during the 1981 crackdown on the emerging movement by a union and other citizens seeking democratic freedoms. The country's then-communist

Although Hubert Sobczynski is a professional sushi chef, he cooks and serves European fare for family and guests (coffee and pastries at the Sobczynscy apartment).

government declared martial law; the military assumed power over civilian activities, and the borders were closed. Food remained scarce throughout the decade. And even when food could be found, there was little money to buy it. "Sometimes, my father would leave in the morning when it was still dark, to see what he could find," Marzena says. "He might not come back until late in the evening, but how happy he was and proud of himself when he came back home with food."

Because of the hardships, the smallest pleasures brought happiness, "even the smallest bar of chocolate, or a mint candy," says Marzena. Now, in these more prosperous times, she worries that her daughter doesn't appreciate how well off she is. "So few things make Klaudia happy," she laments. "Candies are merely candies—nothing is special. Bananas, oranges—they are normal to have. For us, they were something incredibly special, and they still are."

FAMILY RECIPE

Hubert's Knuckle

- 6 pimento berries, dried
- 6 tablespoons salt, plus additional for the soup
- 6 bay leaves
- 4 pig's knuckles
- 2 onions, chopped
- Soup vegetables (carrots, celery, parsnips, turnips)
- 1 or 2 bouillon cubes (optional)
- Pepper

In a deep bowl or pot, add the pimento berries, salt, and 3 bay leaves to 3 quarts of water to make a brine.

Rinse the knuckles well and place them in the brine, making sure they are completely covered. Refrigerate for 3 days. Remove the knuckles and rinse them, discarding the brine.

Fry onions in a dry pan until they are a deep brown, almost black all over (this intensifies the taste and aroma).

In a large soup pot, combine the soup vegetables, bouillon, knuckles, the remaining 3 bay leaves, and salt and pepper to taste with 3 quarts of water. Cook for about 3 hours, until the knuckles are tender.

Serve with bread and either horseradish or mustard.

Turkey THE ÇELIKS OF ISTANBUL

The Çelik family in the main room of their three-room apartment in Istanbul, Turkey, with a week's worth of food. Mêhmêt Çelik, 40, stands between his wife Melahat, 33 (in black), and her mother, Habibe Fatma Kose, 51. Sitting on the couch are their children (back to front) Mêtin, 16, Semra, 15, and Aykut, 8. Cooking method: gas stove. Food preservation: refrigerator-freezer.

ONE WEEK'S FOOD IN JANUARY: 198.48 NEW TURKISH LIRAS/$145.88 USD

Grains and Other Starchy Foods: $10.46
bread, 32 loaves, 49.4 lb, 2 loaves missing • The family
    ate them while waiting for the photograph to be taken.
potatoes, 11 lb
rice, 6.6 lb
yufka (paper-thin pastry sheets), 2.2 lb, purchased from
    a street vendor
Filiz pasta, 1.1 lb

Dairy: $12.16
yogurt, 2.1 qt
feta cheese, in water, 2.2 lb
Dost milk, 1.1 qt
drinkable yogurt (Bandirma style), 1.1 qt
Sana butter, 8.8 oz

Meat, Fish, and Eggs: $11.50
eggs, 24
hamsi (anchovy-like fish), 1.1 lb, generally eaten twice a
    month
beef, 13.2 oz, eaten one or two times a month only • The
    meat shown in the picture is enough for one month.

Fruits, Vegetables, and Nuts: $56.53
oranges, 6.6 lb
tangerines, 6.6 lb
dates,‡ 2.2 lb
yellow bananas, 2.2 lb
pomegranates, 2.1 lb
zucchini, 7.9 lb
tomatoes, 4.4 lb
black olives, 3.3 lb
chickpeas, dried, 3.3 lb
cabbage, 1 head
carrots, 2.2 lb
eggplant, 2.2 lb
leeks, 2.2 lb
lentils, 2.2 lb
lettuce, 2 heads
peppers,‡ 2.2 lb
spinach, 2.2 lb
yellow onions, 2.2 lb
cucumber, 1.7 lb
arugula, 1 lb
Avsarlar nuts, mixed, 2.2 lb

Condiments: $9.60
sunflower oil,‡ 1.1 qt
Bal Küpü white sugar, cubed, 1.1 lb
jam, 10.6 oz
honey, 10.1 fl oz
mint, dried, 8.8 oz
salt, 8 oz
cinnamon, 7.1 oz
pepper, 7.1 oz

Snacks and Desserts: $0.51
Seyidoglu helva (sesame seed paste cookie), 1.1 lb

Prepared Food: $1.36
Knorr Gunun Corbasa dry soup, powdered, 11.2 oz

Homemade Food:
stuffed pastries, approx. 4.4 lb, sheets of *yufka* formed,
    then filled with arugula and feta, listed above
dolmas, approx. 2.2 lb, grape leaves stuffed with spices,
    rice, vegetables, and meat, listed above

Beverages: $29.66
Efes beer, 8 17-fl-oz bottles
Coca-Cola, 8 12-fl-oz cans
Fanta orange soda, 2.1 qt
Hediyelik tea, 3.3 lb
Pepsi, 3 12-fl-oz cans
Coca-Cola light, 12 fl oz
Nescafé VIP instant coffee, 3.5 oz
bottled water, purchased for cooking and drinking

Miscellaneous: $14.10
Tekel cigarettes, 7 packs
Simarik bird food, 20 oz

FACTS ABOUT TURKEY

Population of Istanbul: 8,803,468

Total annual health care expenditure per person
  in US$: $325

Population age 20 and older with diabetes: 7.3%

Population living on less than $2 a day: 19%

Melahat Çelik is assembling the ingredients for *sigara boregi*. The dish is a favorite of her whole family: husband, Mehmet, a factory worker; their three children; and Melahat's mother, Habibe. Melahat seats herself on the living room floor behind her *sofra*, a low, round food-preparation table used in many Turkish homes, which she brought to Istanbul from her hometown. She combines fresh arugula and feta cheese, sets the mixture aside, then unfolds the package of fresh *yufka* (thin pastry sheets), purchased from a nearby street vendor. Laying one sheet across her little table, she rolls it out with a practiced motion, slices it, and plops on a bit of the filling. Using the palm of her hand, she folds the pastry around the filling to make a cigar shape, dips the pastry edge into a water bowl, and lightly presses it against the roll to glue it closed. She keeps rolling out more sheets and dropping in more dollops of the arugula and cheese mixture, until she has a pile of pastries ready for the frying pan.

The preparation of this meal has taken the better part of two

At a neighborhood open-air market, near one of Melahat's housekeeping jobs, she and her son Aykut buy eggs.

Melahat Çelik sits on the living room floor and rolls paper-thin pastry called *yufka* around the filling to create an eggroll-style pastry her family loves.

hours after she's had a long day at work. "Whether I'm tired or not, I cook these same foods," she says. The list includes homemade lentil or tomato soup, rice soup, *dolma* (chopped spiced meat wrapped in grape leaves), spinach, eggplant, zucchini, rice, black cabbage, and occasionally a fish or meat dish like *yahni* (lamb with onions and potato). "My sister Döne sometimes takes care of the children when I'm late at work," says Melahat, "but I do most of the cooking."

Melahat has cleaned other people's homes since the couple got married in the Anatolian city of Kastamonu, in Turkey's Black Sea region, where she and her husband both grew up. As is customary, their families arranged for them to marry. The couple moved to Istanbul almost immediately to find work, and Melahat's widowed mother Habibe followed shortly thereafter. The Çeliks' small one-bedroom apartment is a tight fit for the family of five, plus a grandmother,

Melahat's goal is to see that her three children get enough education so they can avoid the physical labor that she and her husband, both uneducated, must do for a living. "It is okay for me to go hungry, as long as I can afford a good education for [them]," she says. "My children shouldn't live the way I do. It can be a burden to serve or clean up after someone else."

Already her children's lives are quite different from her life in Kastamonu. Her son Mêtin, sixteen, and daughter Semra, fifteen, attend high school and are doing well; Melahat believes they will be able to find good employment. But she is perplexed by her children's attraction to fast food, especially McDonald's. She hears from the people she works for that it isn't healthy to eat such food, but she has trouble telling the children that they can't have it on the few occasions in a year when there might be extra money for a treat. Her eight-year-old son Aykut "likes to have the hamburgers and French fries, to get the little toy gifts they give with the kids' menu," she says. "If I had more money, I'd rather buy chicken and meat every day for my children." But four or five times a year, when she does have the money, she takes them to the McDonald's at the local mall.

On Friday, the noon prayers have begun and a vendor arranges his oranges while behind him men pray at a small mosque.

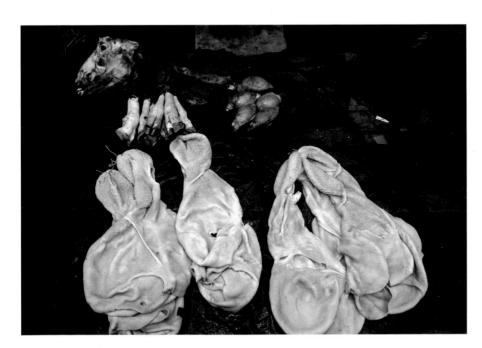

In a market near the Golden Horn, a butcher displays cow stomachs, hearts, livers, feet, and a head.

A fishmonger in an Istanbul market offers a Turkish favorite, the anchovy-like fish *hamsi*, which can be cooked, according to a Black Sea legend, in forty different ways. In his canvas-covered stall, the vendor moves from neighborhood market to neighborhood market, each open a different day of the week.

United States THE CAVENS OF CALIFORNIA

The Caven family in the kitchen of their home in American Canyon, California, with a week's worth of food. Craig Caven, 38 (holding Ryan, 3), and Regan Ronayne, 42, stand behind the kitchen island. In the foreground is Andrea, 5. Cooking methods: electric stove, microwave, outdoor BBQ. Food preservation: refrigerator-freezer, freezer. Favorite foods—Craig: beef stew; Regan: berry yogurt sundae (from Costco); Andrea: clam chowder; Ryan: ice cream.

ONE WEEK'S FOOD IN APRIL: $159.18 USD

Grains and Other Starchy Foods: $30.11
San Luis sourdough bread, sliced, 2 loaves
Oroweat cinnamon raisin bagels, 2.5 lb
Oroweat onion bagels, 2.5 lb
potatoes, 2 lb
Kellogg's raisin bran cereal, 1 lb
Quaker oatmeal, instant, 1 lb
Bohemian Hearth seven-grain bread, sliced, half loaf
No Yolk egg noodles, 12 oz
Mission Gorditas flour tortillas, 10 oz
Buitoni five-cheese tortellini, 8 oz
Pillsbury Best all-purpose flour, 8 oz
Progresso bread crumbs, 4 oz

Dairy: $6.22
Sunny Select (store brand) milk,‡ 1 gal
cheese,‡ shredded, 8 oz
Kraft parmesan cheese, grated, 3 oz

Meat, Fish, and Eggs: $22.87
Foster Farms chicken breast tenders, 4 lb
Sunnyside eggs, 12
beef, ground, 1.5 lb
tuna fish,‡ canned, 1 lb

Fruits, Vegetables, and Nuts: $21.30
Del Monte yellow bananas, 5 lb
Braeburn variety apples, 2.5 lb
Golden Delicious variety apples, 2.5 lb
tangerines, 2 lb
red grapes, 1.5 lb
baby carrots, 2 lb
broccoli, 1 lb
carrots, 1 lb
Sunny Select mixed vegetables, frozen, 8 oz
Sunny Select peas, frozen, 8 oz

Condiments: $9.43
Skippy Roasted Honey Nut peanut butter, 1.1 lb
C&H white cane sugar, 8 oz
Mary Ellen apricot jam, 4 oz
Best Foods mayonnaise,‡ 2 oz
French's yellow mustard,‡ 2 oz
Heinz ketchup,‡ 2 oz
salt, 1.6 oz

Snacks and Desserts: $11.54
Snyders sourdough nibbler pretzels, 1 lb
Sunny Select raisins, 12 oz
Sunny Select vanilla wafers, 12 oz
Sunny Select Blueberry Fruit & Grain cereal bars, 10.4 oz
Sunny Select Raspberry Fruit & Grain cereal bars, 10.4 oz

Prepared Food: $19.33
Red Baron pepperoni pizza, 4 lb
ham submarine sandwiches, 2 12-oz • Craig buys a sandwich at school two times a week.
Foster Farms corn dogs, 1.3 lb
Five Brothers marinara sauce, 12 oz
Rice-A-Roni, chicken flavor, 6.9 oz

Fast Food: $7.50
McDonald's: 2 Happy Meals (each containing 1 6-piece chicken McNuggets, 1 small French fries, 1 low-fat milk)
chocolate chip cookies, 1 package

Restaurants: $4.50
Fresh Choice Restaurant • The family eats here once a month, using a coupon to help defray the cost. Price shown reflects one-fourth of the cost of one visit per month.

Beverages: $22.89
Alhambra water, 5 gal
Coca-Cola,‡ 2.6 qt
diet *Coca-Cola,* 2.2 qt, fountain drinks purchased before daily drive to work
Capri Sun juice drink, 10 6.8-fl-oz packages
apple juice, 2 qt
Tropicana homestyle orange juice, 2 qt
Sunny Select instant coffee, 12 oz
tap water for cooking

Miscellaneous: $3.49
Whiskas Savory Nuggets cat food, 3.3 lb

‡Not in photo

Mexico

United States

On Easter Sunday the kids join Craig's family in Santa Rosa, 45 minutes away, for their annual Easter egg hunt, complete with a man in an Easter Bunny suit.

contributing to the ill health of children: parents aren't teaching their children good eating habits.

Craig and his wife, Regan, a counselor at the University of California, Berkeley, try to find a balance between what their own two children, Andrea, five, and Ryan, three, want and what they actually need. "I don't mind cooking, but I often get home with no time to think about what to cook," says Regan, who commutes an hour to work. Though they have been known to eat a frozen corn dog or two, she doesn't regularly serve convenience food. Despite the time pressure, Regan manages to make a nutritious meal, thanks to her culinary sidekick, the microwave oven. And exercise? Craig says there isn't much

Although states have begun to crack down on the school district practice of allowing students access to vending machines stuffed with sugar-laden drinks and snacks, until recently there were more soft drink machines than water fountains in the Northern California high school where Craig Caven teaches. Soft drink companies and snack vendors provided cash-strapped schools with much-needed funding. Now that there is increased awareness of the alarming rate of childhood overweight and obesity, healthier alternatives like bottled water and juices are being introduced and sugary snacks and drinks are being banned. While this may make a small difference, Craig believes there is a far more pervasive factor

time for it. "I've never been on a diet—although some gentle hints have been made in my direction within the past year or so."

Although Regan and Craig have the same nutritional goals at the grocery store, their approaches to shopping differ. Regan is a self-proclaimed label reader. "I save my reading for home," says Craig. He tries to get into and out of the grocery store as quickly as possible and to buy store brands, because "they're generally cheaper than national brands." Regan is looking for "foods low in sodium, low in fat, not too processed, fresh, and organic, if they're not too expensive."

"My mother didn't have access to the nutrition information now required by the U.S. government," says Regan. "She trusted that if

Soft drink companies and snack vendors provided cash-strapped school districts with much-needed funding.

Momentarily suspending a wrestling match with his son, Craig tilts his head back to share a cartoon moment (left). They are surrounded by debris from the Happy Meals they purchased at the drive-through window of a McDonald's in Napa, California, on the way home from the weekly shopping expedition to Raley's, a California grocery chain (below).

the market carried a food item, it must be okay to eat it. So we ate a lot of time-saving food—packaged and canned—rarely anything fresh. I, on the other hand, rarely feed my family canned foods." She prefers serving fresh fruits and vegetables.

The Cavens generally eat at home, trying to set a good example—though a few times a month they take the children out for Happy Meals. They've found that doing what's right is not always that easy. "There are just too many chocolate holidays," says Regan. "I get through the Christmas candy just in time for Valentine's Day. Next, it's Easter. Then, maybe I can keep away from sweets until Halloween."

The Revis family in the kitchen of their home in suburban Raleigh, North Carolina, with a week's worth of food. Ronald Revis, 39, and Rosemary Revis, 40, stand behind Rosemary's sons from her first marriage, Brandon Demery, 16 (left), and Tyrone Demery, 14. Cooking methods: electric stove, toaster oven, microwave, outdoor BBQ. Food preservation: refrigerator-freezer. Favorite foods—Ronald and Brandon: spaghetti; Rosemary: "potatoes of any kind"; Tyrone: sesame chicken.

ONE WEEK'S FOOD IN MARCH: $341.98 USD

Grains and Other Starchy Foods: $17.92
red potatoes, 2.3 lb
Natures Own bread, sliced, 1 loaf
Trix cereal, 1.5 lb
Mueller fettuccini, 1 lb
Mueller spaghetti, 1 lb
Uncle Ben's Original white rice, 1 lb
Flatout flatbread wraps, 14 oz
New York Original Texas garlic toast, 11.3 oz
Harris Teeter (store brand) Flaky Brown-n-Serve
    dinner rolls, 11 oz

Dairy: $14.51
Harris Teeter milk, 1 gal
Kraft cheese, shredded, 8 oz
Kraft sharp Cheddar cheese, sliced, 8 oz
Kraft Swiss cheese, sliced, 8 oz
Kraft Cheese Singles, 6 oz
Kraft Parmesan cheese, grated, 3 oz
Harris Teeter butter, 2 oz

Meat, Fish, and Eggs: $54.92
Harris Teeter beef pot roast, 2.5 lb
Harris Teeter pork chops, 1.9 lb
Harris Teeter chicken drumsticks, 1.7 lb
eggs, 12
Harris Teeter chicken wings, 1.5 lb
Armour Italian-style meat balls, 1 lb
Gwaltney bacon, Virginia cured with brown sugar, 1 lb
Harris Teeter ground turkey, 1 lb
shrimp,‡ 1 lb
StarKist tuna, canned, 12 oz
honey-baked ham, sliced, 9 oz
smoked turkey, sliced, 7.8 oz

Fruits, Vegetables, and Nuts: $41.07
Dole yellow bananas, 2.9 lb
red seedless grapes, 2.4 lb
green seedless grapes, 2.2 lb
Birds Eye baby broccoli, frozen, 4 lb
yellow onions, 3 lb
Green Giant corn, canned, 1.9 lb
Green Giant green beans, canned, 1.8 lb
Bush's vegetarian baked beans, canned, 1.8 lb
cucumbers, 1.4 lb
Harris Teeter tomatoes, vine-ripened, 1.2 lb
Del Monte whole leaf spinach, canned, 13.5 oz
garden salad, packaged, 10 oz

Italian salad mix, packaged, 8.8 oz
pickled mushrooms, 7.3 oz
Harris Teeter peanuts, 1 lb

Condiments: $12.51
white sugar, 1.6 lb
Ruffles ranch dip, 11 oz
Crisco vegetable oil, 6 fl oz
Nestlé Coffee-Mate, French vanilla, nonfat, 6 fl oz
Food Lion garlic salt, 5.3 oz
Hellmann's mayonnaise, 4 oz
Newman's Own salad dressing, 4 oz
Jiffy peanut butter,‡ 3 oz
black pepper, 2 oz
Harris Teeter Original yellow mustard, 2 oz
Heinz ketchup, 2 oz
salt, 2 oz
Colonial Kitchen meat tenderizer, 1 oz
Durkee celery seed, 1 oz
Encore garlic powder, 1 oz

Snacks and Desserts: $21.27
Mott's apple sauce, 1.5 lb
Munchies Classic mix, 15.5 oz
Kellogg's yogurt-flavored pop tarts,‡ 14.7 oz
Orville Redenbacher's popcorn, 9 oz
Harris Teeter sunflower seeds, 7.3 oz
Lays Classic potato chips, 5.5 oz
Lays Wavy potato chips, 5.5 oz
Del Monte fruit in cherry gel, 4.5 oz
Extra chewing gum, 3 packs
Snickers candy bar, 2.1 oz
M&M's peanut candy, 1.7 oz

Prepared Food: $24.27
Bertolli portobello alfredo sauce, 1 lb
Ragu spaghetti sauce, chunky mushroom and
    bell peppers, 1 lb
Maruchan shrimp-flavored ramen, 15 oz
California sushi rolls, 14 oz
Campbell's cream of celery soup, 10.8 oz
Hot Pockets, jalapeño steak and cheese, 9 oz
shrimp sushi rolls, 7 oz

Fast Food: $71.61
McDonald's: 10-pc chicken McNuggets, large fries, large
    Coca-Cola, Filet-o-Fish meal
Taco Bell: 4 nachos Bell Grande, 2 soft tacos, taco
    supreme, taco pizza, taco, bean burrito, large lemonade

Burger King: double cheeseburger, onion rings, large
    Coca-Cola
KFC: 2-pc chicken with mashed potatoes, large *Coca-Cola*
Subway: 6-inch wheat veggie sub, 6-inch wheat seafood
    crab sub
Milano's Pizzeria: large sausage pizza, large pepperoni
    pizza
I Love NY Pizza: 4 pizza slices

Restaurants: $6.15
China Market: shrimp fried rice, 2 orders; large fruit punch

Beverages: $77.75
Budweiser, 24 12-fl-oz cans
bottled water, 2 gal
Harris Teeter cranberry-apple juice cocktail, 4 2-qt bottles
diet *Coca-Cola*, 12 12-fl-oz cans
A&W cream soda, 2 2.1-qt bottles
7UP, 6 16.9-fl-oz bottles
Harris Teeter cranberry-raspberry juice cocktail,
    2 2-qt bottles
Harris Teeter ruby grapefruit juice cocktail, 2 2-qt bottles
Capri Sun, 10 6.8-fl-oz packages
soda,‡ 5 12-fl-oz cans, purchased daily by Brandon
    at school
Arbor Mist strawberry wine blenders, 1.1 qt
Gatorade,‡ 16 fl-oz bottle
Powerade,‡ 16 fl-oz bottle
Snapple, Go Bananas juice drink, 16 fl oz
Maxwell House instant coffee, 1.5 oz
Kool-Aid, black cherry, 0.5 oz
breakfast tea, 5 teabags
tap water for drinking and cooking

‡Not in photo

FACTS ABOUT THE UNITED STATES

Population age 20 and older with diabetes: 8.8%

**Percent paid by taxpayers for all obesity-related
    medical costs: 50%**

Dieting men/women on any given day: 25/45%

**Annual spending on dieting and diet-related
    products: $40 billion**

**Dieters who will regain their lost weight within
    1 to 5 years: 95%**

The Revis family is living proof that an exhausting schedule does not an exercise program make. As a consumer protection specialist for the North Carolina Department of Justice, Rosemary Revis is busy in the office and equally busy at home, caring for her teenage sons, Brandon and Tyrone, and her husband, Ron. The physical demands are less challenging than the mental ones—a common condition in modern life. After racing through overscheduled days and constantly nibbling, she says, she found herself thirty pounds overweight. Rosemary tried Weight Watchers and shed the pounds, only to gain them back within six months. "I went back to my old eating habits."

Brandon, who's off from school this week, accompanies Rosemary to shop for their week's worth of food (above) for the food portrait at the Harris Teeter supermarket, a short drive from their suburban home. Rosemary chooses a lunchtime sandwich at Subway (left) during the work week, or eats in the State Capital cafeteria.

She wasn't the only family member to struggle with food. When Tyrone, now fourteen, was younger, he was a picky eater. Then his grandmother moved in to help care for the boys. "My mother is a great cook," says Rosemary. "She'd cook things like cube steak with gravy and onions, cabbage, boiled potatoes, and cornbread. She'd fry pork chops and chicken, make collards and fresh salad greens. We'd come home in the evening, and the house would smell delicious. It was a feast." Tyrone became less picky. And as he got older, like most American teens, he was also eating a lot of snacks and fast food and gaining too much

Rosemary Revis's Stuffed Green Peppers

1 pound ground turkey
1 onion, coarsely chopped
6 ounces instant rice, uncooked
3/4 cup water
1 14 1/2-ounce can peeled and diced tomatoes with juice
1 14 1/2-ounce can stewed tomatoes, chopped
Salt
Pepper
1 14 1/2-ounce can corn (optional)
4 large green bell peppers
16 ounces spaghetti sauce
1/2 to 1 pound mozzarella cheese, grated

Brown the ground turkey and onions in a large skillet over medium heat. Drain and discard the fat.

Add the rice, water, diced tomatoes, and stewed tomatoes to the skillet. Season with salt and pepper to taste and simmer until the rice is tender. Add the corn and remove from the heat.

Preheat the oven to 325°F.

Cut the tops off the bell peppers and scrape out the seeds and membrane. Fill the peppers with the meat-rice mixture.

Stand up the peppers in a casserole dish and bake for 25 minutes, or until the peppers are tender.

Just before the time is up, heat up the spaghetti sauce. Remove the peppers from the oven and cover with the sauce. Top with the mozzarella and return to the oven to melt the cheese.

in the winter, basketball and walking during the rest of the year. But he eats fast food for lunch five days a week, and at home "he's a big meat eater," says Rosemary. The workouts were great, but there was an unintentional side effect: they had less time for home-cooked meals. "We would pick up fast food. It was the most convenient thing to do," says Rosemary. "That is not the result that we had in mind when we started this exercise program."

So the family ditched the health club and now uses exercise equipment at home—nearer to the fresh vegetables, leaner meats, and well-planned meals now being served on their dinner table—and they're cutting back on the fast food. The Revises' new fare includes more fresh vegetables and leaner cuts of meat, and they police one another's refrigerator habits. "Before Brandon eats something now," says Rosemary, "he'll say to me, 'Mom, how much fat do you think is in that sandwich?' That never happened before."

The Revis family's two-hour exercise session at the local health club (foreground, Brandon curling weights; background, left to right, Rosemary, Tyrone, and Ron).

weight. "I would just sit on the couch and watch TV and eat—hot pockets, burritos, fried eggs," he says. He began spending more time on his skateboard, but the call of the potato chip was still mighty and strong. When his mother—determined to lose weight—joined a health club, he joined too. So did Ron and Brandon. Ron, a trim, fit man, works out mainly for the cardio benefits, he says—treadmill

United States THE FERNANDEZES OF TEXAS

The Fernandez family in the kitchen of their San Antonio, Texas, home with a week's worth of food—Lawrence, 31, and wife, Diana, 35, standing, and Diana's mother, Alejandrina Cepeda, 58, sitting with her grandchildren Brian, 5, and Brianna, 4. Cooking methods: electric stove, microwave, toaster oven, outdoor BBQ. Food preservation: refrigerator-freezer. Favorite foods—Diana: shrimp with Alfredo sauce; Lawrence: barbecue ribs; Brian and Brianna: pizza; Alejandrina: chicken mole.

ONE WEEK'S FOOD IN MARCH: $242.48 USD

Grains and Other Starchy Foods: $19.28
potatoes, 5 lb
homemade tortillas, 1.6 lb
Kellogg's Special K cereal with red berries, 1.5 lb
Nature's Own honey wheat bread, 1 loaf
Quaker masa harina, 1.3 lb
Gold Medal all-purpose flour, 1 lb
H-E-B (store brand) French-style bread, 1 lb
white rice, 1 lb
Cream of Wheat cereal, 14 oz
Quaker oatmeal, 13.5 oz
dinner rolls, 13 oz
Post Cocoa Pebbles cereal, 13 oz
H-E-B fettuccine, 5.3 oz
Q&Q vermicelli, 5 oz

Dairy: $17.72
Borden Kid Builder milk, 1% low fat, high calcium, 1 gal
Oak Farms Skim Deluxe milk, 1 gal
Blue Bell ice cream, 1 qt
Danon Danimals, Swingin' Strawberry Banana and Rockin' Raspberry drinkable yogurt, 25.2 fl oz
Yoplait piña colada yogurt, 1.5 lb
Yoplait blueberry yogurt, 12 oz
Kraft Colby and Monterey Jack cheese, 8 oz
Frigo Cheese Heads string cheese, 6 oz

Meat, Fish, and Eggs: $42.10
Hill Country Fare chicken drumsticks, 3 lb
Hill Country Fare jumbo eggs, 18
H-E-B rotisserie chicken, original flavor, 2.5 lb
Sanderson Farms chicken thigh fillets, boneless and skinless, 1.5 lb
Gorton's Original Tenders fish sticks, frozen, 1.1 lb
H-E-B extra-lean beef, ground, 1 lb
H-E-B turkey breast, ground, 1 lb
Oscar Mayer turkey cotto salami, 1 lb
shrimp, frozen, 1 lb
Butterball turkey variety pack, sliced, 12 oz
H-E-B beef, top round cubes, 12 oz
Tyson fun nuggets, frozen chicken, 12 oz
Hill Country Fare smoked chicken, sliced, 5 oz

Fruits, Vegetables, and Nuts: $33.05
grapefruit, 5 lb
Dole bananas, 2.5 lb
Granny Smith apples, 1.3 lb
green grapes, 1.3 lb

Coastal strawberries, 1 lb
Key limes, 1 lb
red apples, 12.8 oz
Hass avocados, 4
Hunts tomato sauce, 2.5 lb
Green Giant green beans, canned, 2 lb
Green Giant corn, frozen, 1.6 lb
tomatoes, 1.3 lb
La Sierra refried pinto beans, 15 oz
iceberg lettuce, 1 head
Fresh Express Italian salad mix, 8.8 oz
yellow onions, 8.6 oz
Fresh Express coleslaw, 8 oz
mini carrots, 8 oz
mushrooms, sliced, 8 oz
jalapeño peppers, 4 oz
garlic, 2 oz
Planters honey-roasted peanuts, 12 oz

Condiments: $16.05
Great Value vegetable oil, 2.1 qt
Hill Country Fare BBQ sauce, 1.1 lb
International Delight coffee creamer, 16 fl oz
I Can't Believe It's Not Butter spread, 15.8 oz
Aunt Jemima Butter Lite syrup, 12 oz
Hill Country Fare ketchup, 9 oz
Clover Burleson's honey, 8 oz
H-E-B roasted pepper salsa picante, 8 oz
Season All seasoned salt, 8 oz
Wish-Bone Classic Ranch-Up! dressing, 6 oz
peanut butter, 4 oz
pepper, ground, 1 oz
salt, 0.5 oz

Snacks and Desserts: $23.33
H-E-B Texas-shaped corn chips, 1 lb
pretzels, 1 lb
Dreyers whole-fruit bar popsicles, 16.5 fl oz
Oreo cookies, 9 oz
Ritz whole wheat crackers, 7.5 oz
Pepperidge Farm Goldfish Colors crackers, 6.6 oz
Ritz Sticks crackers, 6.3 oz
Pringles potato chips, 6 oz
General Mills Fruit Gushers snacks, 5.4 oz
Kellogg's Special K blueberry bars, 4.9 oz
Kellogg's Special K peaches and berry bars, 4.9 oz
Orville Redenbacher's Smart Pop microwave popcorn, 3.7 oz
Barnum's animal crackers, 2.1 oz

Prepared Food: $18.16
Prego spaghetti sauce, 1 lb
La Sierra refried beans with cheese, 15 oz
Ranch Style beans with jalapeño peppers, 15 oz
Pioneer Brand buttermilk pancake mix, 10.7 oz
Bertolli creamy alfredo sauce, 8 oz
Zatarain's black beans and rice, 7 oz
Zatarain's gumbo mix, 7 oz
Pioneer brown gravy mix, nonfat, 2.8 oz
Pioneer Country gravy mix, nonfat, 2.8 oz
Knorr Suiza chicken broth, 2 oz
Diana at work, 5 cafeteria meals, variety of main courses available; Lawrence at work, a salad or slice of pizza

Fast Food: $11.81
McDonald's: 3 Happy Meals
4 Mountain Blast ice cream drinks
1 vanilla ice cream cone

Restaurants: $42.11
Fire Mountain Buffet: dinner for 5, assorted items, sold by the pound, 3.8 lb
Cici's Pizza: large beef pizza, large white pizza, large meat lover's pizza, 3 salads

Beverages: $18.87
Hill Country Fare natural spring water, 8 gal
Tree Top apple juice, 1 gal
Capri Sun Mountain Cooler, 10 6.8-fl-oz packages
Capri Sun orange drink, 10 6.8-fl-oz packages
Dole pineapple-orange-banana juice, 8 6-fl-oz cartons
Hill Country Fare iced tea mix, 1.7 lb
Wyler's Light pink lemonade, powdered mix, 1.2 lb
H-E-B Café Ole coffee, 3 oz
Ovaltine malted instant drink mix, 3 oz
Kool-Aid, sugar-free grape powdered mix, 1.2 oz

The Fernandezes begin their Sunday grocery trip after lunch. Clutching their spending money, Brianna and Brian head for the bakery case, where they settle on giant *pan dulces*.

languages seamlessly, helping her children understand words they don't know. The conversation is wide-ranging. "What is *limón*?" Brianna asks at one point, as her grandmother hands her a ball of dough. "Lemon," says Diana, as she watches Brian pummel the dough in his press. "Is this pancake okay?" Brianna asks. *"Bueno,"* says Alejandrina, who's expertly pressing most of the tortillas in her own large press. "But it's not a pancake—it's a tortilla," she says in Spanish. Diana translates. Alejandrina will forgo cooking

lejandrina Cepeda works as a nanny on the weekdays, but for an hour on Saturday afternoons she transforms the home she shares with her daughter's family into a Mexican *tortillería*. Her grandchildren stand on chairs with their own kid-size tortilla presses and watch her mix masa harina (corn-flour mix) and water with her hands. Brianna, four, leans over the bowl inquisitively, speaking with her grandmother in English. Alejandrina, who speaks English, answers in her native Spanish. Brian, five, loudly flings his press open and closed several times. "Remember, Brian," warns his mother, Diana Fernandez, a school librarian, "your grandmother likes you to be serious when you're cooking with her." Brian is more interested in eating the tortillas than making them, but with the just-add-water tortilla mix from the supermarket, the process is quick. Diana—who was raised by Alejandrina in the Mexican city of Nuevo Laredo, on the U.S.-Mexico border—flows between the two

the tortillas on a *comal*, a traditional griddle. She'll cook them on the stove and turn them into the kids' favorite—cheese quesadillas.

The Fernandezes eat from the global dinner table most of the time. "We go from mullet to *menudo* to egg rolls," says Diana's husband Lawrence, an accomplished cook who grew up in Louisiana. He credits his upbringing there with sparking his love of food: "When someone invites you to dinner in Louisiana, you never say no. It's going to be a big deal—a big pot of something," says Lawrence. "Especially if they've got a [Creole name like] Breaux or Mouton." Lawrence, who manages a Cici's Pizzeria, also cooks with the children. On those occasions he, too, helps them prepare balls of dough, though ones that are much bigger than his mother-in-law's. "I'll bring raw dough and sauce home," he says, "and the kids and I will build pizzas. And that's a big treat." Any dessert? "Ice cream at midnight, when the kids are asleep."

Diana Fernandez's Quesadillas from Fresh Corn Tortillas

1¹/₂ cups warm water

¹/₄ teaspoon salt

2 cups masa harina (dried, lime-treated fine cornmeal)

4 cups coarsely grated Colby Jack cheese (can substitute any kind of
   Cheddar cheese)

Knead the warm water and salt into the masa harina until the dough is warm and only slightly sticky. Cut the dough into about 18 little balls, each of which will form one tortilla.

Flatten the little dough balls with a *tortillera* (tortilla press) until they are very thin. (They can be rolled with a rolling pin, but this is much more difficult.)

Place a flattened dough circle on a seasoned *comal* (a flat cooking pan made specially to cook tortillas) on medium-high heat.

Once the tortilla yellows and becomes harder, put a handful of cheese in the middle and fold the tortilla in half. Keep the folded tortilla on the *comal* just long enough to melt the cheese, turning it over when necessary (about 5 minutes total).

Serve immediately.

After the Saturday soccer game, Diana and Alejandrina perform a family ritual (left): making fresh tortillas (in background) for cheese quesadillas (see recipe above). The next day, though, it's back to less less-than-traditional fare: takeout chicken and soda pop (top).

At home, Brian polishes off a cheeseburger from Whataburger (above).

FURTHER READING

BOOKS

Animal, Vegetable, Miracle: A Year of Food Life by Barbara Kingsolver (HarperCollins, 2007). The author and her family chronicle a year of procuring as much of their food as possible from local farms and their own backyard.

Chew On This: Everything You Don't Want to Know about Fast Food by Eric Schlosser (Houghton Mifflin, 2007). This fascinating and sometimes frightening truth about "what lurks between those sesame-seed buns" includes excerpts from *Fast Food Nation* and other writings.

Fast Food (At Issue Series) by Tracy Brown Collins (Greenhaven Press, 2004). An anthology that explores the various aspects of the fast food debate.

Fast Food Nation by Eric Schlosser (Harper Perennial, 2005). This searing portrayal of the fast-food industry led readers of all ages to question their meal-time choices.

Fields of Plenty: A Farmer's Journey in Search of Real Food and the People Who Grow It by Michael Ableman (Chronicle Books, 2005). The story of a farmer and his son's journey across the United States in search of innovative farmers and farming methods that are making a difference in what we eat and how we experience food.

Man Eating Bugs by Peter Menzel and Faith D'Aluisio (Material World Books, 1998). This photographic collection studies the art and science of eating insects.

Twinkie, Deconstructed: My Journey to Discover How the Ingredients Found in Processed Foods Are Grown, Mined (Yes, Mined), and Manipulated into What America Eats by Steve Ettlinger (Hudson Street Press, 2007). This book tours the curious world of packaged food and demystifies some of America's most common processed food ingredients.

FILMS

The Future of Food (Lily Films, 2004). Directed by Deborah Koons Garcia; this film explores the genetic modification of foods and their introduction into the world's food supply.

Super Size Me (Kathbur Pictures, 2004). Directed by Morgan Spurlock; the filmmaker documents the effects of a month-long, strictly fast-food diet.

WEBSITES

Center for Food Safety (www.centerforfoodsafety.org)
This nonprofit public interest and environmental advocacy organization challenges harmful food production technologies and promotes sustainable alternatives. Current campaigns include genetically engineered food, cloned animals, sewage sludge, and mad cow disease.

Cool Food Planet (www.coolfoodplanet.org)
Food and nutrition information for teens, kids, parents, and schools from the European Food Information Council. Take a nutrition quiz, learn about the connections between emotions and eating habits, and construct healthy diets to benefit different parts of your body and different lifestyles. Available in several different languages.

Ecological Footprint Quiz (www.globalfootprint.org)
The Ecological Footprint (a tool of The Global Footprint Network) measures how much land and water a human population needs to sustain its lifestyle. Take a quiz to find out how big your own footprint is—how many acres of land and other resources are needed to sustain what you eat and how you live, and how many planets we'd need if everyone in the world lived like you.

Feeding Minds, Fighting Hunger (www.feeding minds.org/yw/index_en.htm)
This United Nations-backed organization inspires youth to join in the fight against hunger.

Friends of the World Food Program (www.friendsof wfp.org)
This U.S.-based nonprofit organization works to increase public awareness of global hunger issues and builds support for the UN's World Food Program and other hunger relief efforts.

Heifer International (www.heifer.org)
A hunger aid program with tons of projects around the world that help families become food self-sufficient and economically stable.

OneWorld.net (us.oneworld.net/guides/food)
This global information network publishes U.S. and international perspectives on global issues. Its range of thematic guides includes a Food Security Guide with an overview of food security, hunger, and nutrition around the world.

Shaping America's Youth (www.shapingamericas youth.com)
Helpful resources and information on the latest and most comprehensive programs across the United States aimed at helping youth improve nutrition and physical activity.

Slow Food USA (www.slowfoodusa.org)
This nonprofit organization educates people about how their food choices affect the rest of the world. Their Slow Food in Schools program empowers students to make informed choices about what they eat.

TeensHealth: advice about food and fitness (www .kidshealth.org/teen/food_fitness)
Nutrition basics, support for reaching and maintaining a healthy weight, fundamentals of healthy exercise, and more sponsored by the Nemours Foundation.

USDA Food and Nutrition Information Center (fnic .nal.usda.gov)
Practical resources about nutrition and food safety.

USDA's Team Nutrition (teamnutrition.usda.gov)
Training, nutrition information, and school and community support for helping youth improve eating habits and physical activity.

What the World Eats (www.whattheworldeats.com)
Additional information and links from the authors of this book.

World Food Day (www.worldfooddayusa.org)
This worldwide event celebrated on October 16 each year is designed to increase awareness, understanding, and informed, year-around action to alleviate hunger.

The World Food Programme (www.wfp.org)
The United Nations frontline agency in the fight against global hunger.

SOURCES

AUSTRALIA

Population: Riverview, Queensland Department of Housing

Land that is desert: University of New South Wales School of Biological Science

Ratio of sheep to people: Meat and Livestock Australia

Indigenous population: Australian Bureau of Statistics 2006

Indigenous population in 1777: Indigenous Australia 2007

Life expectancy gap between indigenous and nonindigenous population: UNDP *2004 Human Development Report*

Per capita total expenditure on health (at average exchange rate): World Health Organization 2004

Kangaroos killed under commercial harvest for meat and skins: Australian Department of the Environment and Water Resources

BHUTAN

Population of Shingkhey Village: Estimated from firsthand observation

Percentage of population that is subsistence farmers: EM Research Organization

Land that is above 10,000 feet in elevation: Food and Agriculture Organization of the UN

Population with access to electricity: BBC News

Per capita total expenditure on health (at average exchange rate): World Health Organization 2004

Number of fast food restaurants: McDonalds.com, BurgerKing.com, PizzaHut.com, and KFC.com (2007)

TV stations in 1998/2005: BBC News

BOSNIA AND HERZEGOVINA

Population of Sarajevo: Bosnia and Herzegovina Federal Office of Statistics 2006

Percentage of population that is undernourished: UNDP *2006 Human Development Report*

Per capita total expenditure on health (at average exchange rate): World Health Organization 2004

Annual sugar and sweetener consumption per capita: Food and Agriculture Organization of the UN 2003

CHAD

Population of Dar Es Salaam: Estimated from firsthand observation

Percentage of population that is subsistence farmers and cattle herders: CIA *World Factbook 2004*

Land planted in permanent crops: CIA *World Factbook 2004*

Percentage of population with sustainable access to an improved water source: UNDP 2006 *Human Development Report*

Years of ethnic warfare endured since gaining independence from France in 1960: *World Factbook 2004*

Physicians per 100,000 people: UNDP 2006 *Human Development Report*

Percentage of population that is undernourished: UNDP 2006 *Human Development Report*

Households with access to electricity: *African Energy* newsletter

Number of fast food restaurants: McDonalds.com, BurgerKing.com, PizzaHut.com, and KFC.com (2007)

CHINA

Population of Metro Beijing: China.org (2005)

Population of Weitaiwu Village: Estimated from firsthand observation and with help of translator

Per capita total expenditure on health (at average exchange rate): World Health Organization 2004

Percentage of population age 20 and above with diabetes: World Health Organization

Annual sugar and sweetener consumption per capita: Food and Agriculture Organization of the UN 2003

Number of KFC restaurants: China Chain Store & Franchise Association (2007)

Population living on less than $2 a day: UNDP 2006 *Human Development Report*

Number of days of curing after which a "thousand-year-old egg" is most delectable: *Food in China: A Cultural and Historical Inquiry* by Frederick J. Simoons (CRC Press, 1991)

Rural population (people/households): China Statistics Bureau

Percentage of laborers in China engaged in agriculture work: Ministry of Agriculture of the People's Republic of China

Population with access to safe water and sanitation in rural/urban areas: Unicef 2004

Ratio of percentage of rural to urban population that is overweight: Worldwatch Institute

Ratio of rural to urban electricity use per person: Program on Energy and Sustainable Development, Stanford, 2004

Ratio of rural to urban household consumption: *China Statistical Yearbook 2003*

Average per capita income, rural/urban: National Bureau of Statistics of China 2007

Number of refrigerators per 100 families: *China and World Economy*

Percentage of rural residential energy consumption that comes from noncommercial sources, that is, straw, paper, dung: The Chinese Academy of Social Sciences

Ratio of internet users in rural/urban areas: China Internet Network Information Center (2007)

DARFUR REGION, SUDAN

Percentage of Darfur population that is refugees within Darfur: International Crisis Group

Sudanese refugee population in Chad: USAID 2005

Population of Breidjing Refugee Camp: UN High Commission for Refugees

U.S. Government aid to Darfur region since 2004: USAID

Number of refugee camps in eastern Chad: World Health Organization

Number of refugee camps in Darfur: USAID

Camels exported from Sudan to Egypt annually for meat: *Al Ahram Weekly Online*

ECUADOR

Population of Tingo village: Estimated from firsthand observation and with help from translator

Indigenous population: U.S. Department of State (2007)

Percentage of population that is undernourished: UNDP 2006 *Human Development Report*

Per capita total expenditure on health (at average exchange rate): World Health Organization 2004

Number of volcanoes: Volcano World

Annual sugar and sweetener consumption per capita: Food and Agriculture Organization of the UN 2003

Population living on less than $2 a day: UNDP 2006 *Human Development Report*

EGYPT

Population of Cairo: www.citypopulation.de

Population with access to electricity: Africa Energy Forum

Percentage of population that is undernourished: UNDP 2006 *Human Development Report*

Per capita total expenditure on health (at average exchange rate): World Health Organization 2004

Percentage of population age 20 and above with diabetes: World Health Organization

Annual sugar and sweetener consumption per capita: Food and Agriculture Organization of the UN 2003

Population living on less than $2 a day: UNDP 2006 *Human Development Report*

Percentage of camels imported into Egypt that is used for food: experts.about.com

FRANCE

Population of Metro Paris: National Institute for Demographic Studies (2006)

Percentage of Paris population that is foreign born: UNDP 2004 *Human Development Report*

Annual per capita consumption of wine/soft drinks: CBC News; www.nutraingredients.com

Per capita total expenditure on health (at average exchange rate): World Health Organization 2004

Cheese consumption per person per year: Elsevier Food International

GREAT BRITAIN

Population of Collingbourne Ducis: Information from the Bainton family

Per capita total expenditure on health (at average exchange rate): World Health Organization 2004

Percentage of population age 20 and above with diabetes: World Health Organization

Fish and chips restaurants: www.plaiceandchips. co.uk

Fish served in fish and chips restaurants per year: www.plaiceandchips.co.uk

GREENLAND

Population of Cap Hope: Firsthand observation and information from the Madsen family

Native Inuit population: Statistics Greenland (2007)

Aid from Denmark per person per year: CIA *World Factbook 2007*

Land not covered in ice: Statistics Greenland (2007)

Total annual health care expenditure per person: NOMESCO Statistics (2005)

Population age 35 and older with diabetes; sugar consumption: Chief Medical Officer for 2003

Percentage of population that eats seal 4 times a week: Danish Environmental Protection Agency

Year that a Greenlandic iceberg sank the *Titanic*: www.factmonster.com

GUATEMALA

Population of Todos Santos de Cuchamatán: www. cause.ca

Indigenous population: UNDP 2004 *Human Development Report*

Rural households with access to electricity: ENCOVI Living Standard Measurement Study

Life expectancy gap between indigenous and nonindigenous population: UNDP 2004 *Human Development Report*

Per capita total expenditure on health (at average exchange rate): World Health Organization 2004

Percentage of population that is undernourished: UNDP 2006 *Human Development Report*

Percentage of population age 20 and above with diabetes: World Health Organization

Population living on less than $2 a day: UNDP 2004 *Human Development Report*

INDIA

Population of Ujjain: Office of the Registrar General and Census Commissioner, India

Per capita total expenditure on health (at average exchange rate): World Health Organization 2004

Physicians per 100,000 people: UNDP 2006 *Human Development Report*

Number of vegetarian Pizza Huts in the world and in India: www.rediff.com

Population living on less than $2 a day: UNDP 2006 *Human Development Report*

Percentage of population that is undernourished: UNDP 2006 *Human Development Report*

Population with access to safe sanitation: UNDP 2006 *Human Development Report*.

JAPAN

Population of Metro Tokyo: Statistical Handbook of Japan 2004; Kodaira City: Kodaira City government

Per capita total expenditure on health (at average exchange rate): World Health Organization 2004

Percentage of population age 20 and above with diabetes: World Health Organization

Fish consumption per person per year: Food and Agriculture Organization of the UN

KUWAIT

Population of Kuwait City: National Geographic (2007)

Percentage of population that is nonnationals: CIA *World Factbook 2004*

Year women were given the right to vote: BBC News

Land that is barren desert: www.gulflink.osd.mil

Water supply from desalinated sea water: www. gulflink.osd.mil

Water supply from brackish ground water: www. gulflink.osd.mil

Food imported: Kuwait Information Office

Oil exported: Kuwait Information Office

Per capita total expenditure on health (at average exchange rate): World Health Organization 2004

Percentage of population age 20 and above with diabetes: World Health Organization

MALI

Population of Kouakourou village: Estimated from firsthand observation

Population living below the poverty line: CIA *World Factbook 2007*

Percentage of population that is nomadic: CIA *World Factbook 2007*

Percentage of population that is farmers or fishermen: CIA *World Factbook 2007*

Land that is desert or semidesert: CIA *World Factbook 2007*

Rural households with access to electricity: Foundation for Rural Energy Services (2007)

Per capita total expenditure on health (at average exchange rate): World Health Organization 2004

Physicians per 100,000 people: UNDP 2006 *Human Development Report*

Percentage of population age 20 and above with diabetes: World Health Organization

Population living on less than $2 a day: UNDP 2006 *Human Development Report*

MEXICO

Population of Cuernavaca: Citypopulation.de (2007)

Indigenous population: UNDP 2004 *Human Development Report*

Life expectancy gap between indigenous and nonindigenous population: UNDP 2004 *Human Development Report*

Per capita total expenditure on health (at average exchange rate): World Health Organization 2004

Percentage of population age 20 and above with diabetes: World Health Organization

Tortilla consumption per person per year: www.signonsandiego.com

Number of restaurants/retail stores run by Walmex: MoneyNews.com (2006)

World rank for per-person consumption of Coca-Cola: Worldwatch Institute

Population living on less than $2 a day: UNDP 2006 *Human Development Report*

MONGOLIA

Population of Ulaanbaatar: National Geographic (2007)

Livestock population: Food and Agriculture Organization of the UN

Number of livestock deaths from drought and *zud* between summer of 1999 and winter of 2002: www.freedomhouse.org

Land used for grazing: Food and Agriculture Organization of the UN

Population living in *gers*: World Health Organization (2005)

Rank of Ulaanbaatar among the world's coldest capitals: Asian Development Bank

Year in which Soviet economic aid stopped: CIA *World Factbook 2007*

Per capita total expenditure on health (at average exchange rate): World Health Organization 2004

Percentage of population age 20 and above with diabetes: World Health Organization

Population living on less than $2 a day: UNDP 2006 *Human Development Report*

PHILIPPINES

Filipinos living or working overseas: *Occidental Quarterly*

Population of Metro Manila: www.absoluteast-ronomy.com

Per capita total expenditure on health (at average exchange rate): World Health Organization 2004

Percentage of population age 20 and above with diabetes: World Health Organization

Number of Jollibee restaurants: www.jollibee.com

Population living on less than $2 a day: UNDP 2006 *Human Development Report*

POLAND

Population of Konstancin-Jeziorna: www.ville-st-germain-en-laye.fr

Per capita total expenditure on health (at average exchange rate): World Health Organization 2004

The Itanoni Tortillería in Oaxaca, Mexico, sells handmade tortillas cooked on top of clay ovens. It contracts with local growers to produce increasingly rare native varieties of corn. Oaxaca is the center of diversity for corn—the world headquarters, so to speak, of its gene pool.

Percentage of population age 20 and above with diabetes: World Health Organization

TURKEY

Population of Istanbul: State Institute of Statistics, Republic of Turkey

Per capita total expenditure on health (at average exchange rate): World Health Organization 2006

Percentage of population age 20 and above with diabetes: World Health Organization

Population living on less than $2 a day: UNDP 2006 *Human Development Report*

UNITED STATES

Caloric intake available from animal products: Food and Agriculture Organization of the UN (2003)

GDP: CIA World Factbook (2006)

Per capita total expenditure on health (at average exchange rate): World Health Organization 2004

Physicians per 100,000 people: UNDP 2006 *Human Development Report*

Annual sugar and sweetener consumption per capita: Food and Agriculture Organization of the UN 2003

Soft drink consumption/Coca-Cola product consumption per person per year: www.mattoni-granddrink.com

Beef/potatoes purchased annually by McDonald's: *New York Times*

Manure from all intensive farming practices per year: Animal Alliance of Canada

Household food waste per year: www.endhunger.org

Cost of household food waste per year: *Medical News Today*

Household food waste per year as a percentage of food purchases: *Medical News Today*

Percentage of population age 20 and above with diabetes: World Health Organization

Percentage paid by taxpayers for obesity-related medical costs: Center for Disease Control

Percentage of dieting men/women on any given day: National Eating Disorders Association

Annual spending on dieting and diet-related products: National Eating Disorders Association

Percentage of all dieters who will regain their lost weight within 1 to 5 years: National Eating Disorders Association

INDEX

A market vendor at Galewela, Sri Lanka, relaxes among his grains and spices while waiting for customers.

ACKNOWLEDGMENTS

A book whose subjects live in twenty-one countries scattered around the world could not have been done without the help of hundreds of people. We are grateful to them all. Our special thanks to the families in this book who opened their homes, hearts, and refrigerators.

Educational consultation: Martha Jackson, Joy Shioshita, Linda A. Perkins, and Linda Hiam

Developmental editing, copyediting, and proofreading: Anne Dunn, Kristi Hein, and Leslie Evans

Recipe testing: Kate Washington

Indexing: Sandi Schroeder

Special thanks to: David Griffin; Charles C. Mann; Ruth Eichhorn and *GEO* magazine, Germany; Nozomu Makino and NHK TV, Japan; Kathleen Strong and Chizuru Nishida, World Health Organization; Sissi Marini, UNDP, New York; Aida Albina and Cedric Bezin, UNHCR, Abeche

Ten Speed Press and Tricycle Press: Phil Wood, Nicole Geiger, Lorena Jones, Julie Bennett, Nancy Austin, Molly Woodward, Katy Brown, Mary Ann Anderson, Laura Mancuso, and Hayley Gonnason

Copia, the American Center for Wine, Food, and the Arts

Pictopia: Mark Liebman, Bryan Bailey, James Cacciatore, and Bo Blanton (www.pictopia.com)

Website: Bo Blanton and Adam Guerrieri

Peter Menzel Photography staff, recent past and present: Liddy Tryon, Sheila DS Foraker, Colleen Leyden D'Aluisio

Australia
Fiona Rowe
Kelly Debono
Val Brown
Bernadette Jeffries
Vic Cherikoff
Beryl Van Oploo
Norma Scott-Molloy

Bhutan
Brent Olson at Geographic
    Expeditions: www.GeoEx.com
Ugen Rinzen at Yangphel Travels:
    www.yangphel.com
Karma Lotey
Yangzom
Yosushi Yugi
Jigme Singye
Tshering Phuntsho
Sha Phurba Dorji
Chato Namgay

Bosnia
Mirha Kuljuh
Mr. Oska
Sheila DS Foraker
Nedzad Eminagic
Arina and Nadja Bucalovic
Lokman Demirovic
Alexandra Boulat

Chad
Aida Albina
Cédric Bezin
Willem Botha
Colin Pryce
Guy Levine
Colin Sanders
Jean Charles Dei
Taban Lokonga
Stefano Porotti
Khamis Hassan Jouma
Eduardo Cué
Nancy Palus
Moustapha Abdelkarim
Hassane Mahamat Senoussi
Stefanie Frease
Abakar Saleh

China
Angela Yu
Joshua N. D'Aluisio-Guerrieri
Leong Ka Tai
Juliet Hsu

Ecuador
Oswaldo Muñoz at
    www.nuevomundotravel.com
David Muñoz
Pablo and Augusto Corral Vega
Cornelia at Simiatug Sinai

Egypt
Mounir and Wagdi Fahmy
Mona Abdel Zaher
Mohamed Bakr of Mitsco
    Languages and Translation:
    www.mitsco.com.eg

France
Isabelle and Pierre Gillet
Annie Boulat and Cosmos
Olivier Dumont
Patrice Lanoy
Delphine Le Moine
Edward Arckless
Rémi Blemia

Great Britain
Philippe Achache
Zute Lightfoot
Michael and Caroline Martin

Greenland
Knud Brinkløv Jensen
Lars Pederson
Karina Bernlow and Marten
    Munck at Nanu Travel:
    www.nanu-travel.com
Kathleen Cartwright at
    Arcturus Expeditions:
    www.arcturusexpeditions.co.uk

Guatemala
Naomi Robertson
Pablo Perez
Eve Astrid Andersson

India
Neha Diddee
Susan Welchman
Manoj Davey
William Allard
Kathy Moran

Japan
Hui-ling Sun
Toyoo Ohta
Lina Wang
John Tsui
Asaka Barsley
Hsiu-lin Wang
Hirofumi Ando

Kuwait
Bill Kalis
Michel Stephenson
Haider Farman
Larry Flak
Brian Krause
Aisa BouYabes
Sara Akbar

Mali
Patricia Minn
Kone Lassine
Albert Gano
Sékou Macalou

Mexico
Juan Espinosa
Agustin Gutierrez
Angélica Pardiñas Romero
Mauricio Casteñeda
Jorge Vasquez Villalón
T. Boone Hallberg
Amada Ramirez Leyva
Lea Gabriela Fernandez Orantes
Irma Ortiz Perez

Mongolia
Tanya Suren
Tuvshin Mend at
    www.mogultravel.mn

Philippines
Elaine Capili
Peter Ginter

Poland
Ewa, Borys, and Ola Ledochowicz
Dorota and Bartek Waśniewscy
Malgorzata Maruszkin
Albert Krako

Turkey
Ferit Kayabal
Ugurlu Yaltir
Sezgi & Feriye

USA
Ray Kinoshita
Melanie Lawson
John Guess
Dawn D'Aluisio
Karen and Bob Prior
Malena Gonzales-Cid
Lisa Kuny
Ellie Menzel
Linda and Ron Junier
Ruben Perez
Paul Franson
Brian Braff
Nicole David
Miriam Hernandez
Andrew Clarke
Linda Dallas
Billy and Kimberly Campbell
Philip Greenspun
Michael Hawley
JP Caldwell, for taking care of Oscar
    during our many absences

```
YA          Menzel, Peter,
641.3       1948-

MENZEL      What the world eats.


            23.00
$22.99                  11/18/2009
```

DATE			

BAKER & TAYLOR